ST. ANDREWS
PRESBYTERIAN CHURCH
8190 LINCOLN RD.
BEULAH, MI 49617

Blessed are the Peacemakers

The Story of Archbishop Elias Chacour
Another Man from Galilee and Peacemaker in Israel / Palestine

Patricia R. Griggs with Archbishop Elias Chacour

For information
Visit our Website: www.pilgrimsofibillin.org

Bible references are from the New Revised Standard Version of the Bible

Photography
Members of the Vineyard Chapter of Pilgrims of Ibillin, Livermore, CA
and archives of Elias Chacour

Copyright © 2012 by Pilgrims of Ibillin
All rights reserved

Dedication

This book is dedicated to the students and wonderful faculty of Mar Elias Educational Institutions.

May your dreams of justice and a bright future for all, Arab and Jew, come true.

Acknowledgements

No book is written in isolation. I wish to thank Abuna Elias Chacour for sharing his stories with me, and his affirmation of the way I have presented his story. I appreciate his encouragement to write this book, and especially his friendship.

I wish to express a big thank you to the students and faculty at Mar Elias Educational institutions (MEEI) for their friendship. They have opened their hearts and offered incredible hospitality whenever I have come to visit. Their dedication to peace and hope for the future has been inspiring.

I was nearly done with the manuscript when Elias Abu Ghanima came to the United States to raise money for MEEI. As I traveled with Elias to fund raising events and listened to his stories, I realized that many of them should be included. Thank you Elias for allowing me to share the wonderful stories of the Mar Elias graduates and for the efforts you made when you returned to Israel to obtain some of the old photographs from the archives.

My friend and husband, Donald, has encouraged, edited, and contributed to the book in many ways. I am indebted to him for the contributions he made and thank him for his loving support.

Thank you to my friends Nancy Mikoski and Carol Wehrheim for sharing one of the first drafts of this book with their 5th and 6th graders at Nassau Presbyterian Church in Princeton, New Jersey. The feedback they gave me and suggestions for improving the book inspired me. I am grateful for such good friends.

Patricia Griggs

Contents

Foreword			5
Introduction			7
Greetings			9
Chapter	1	My Home — Biram	12
Chapter	2	Trouble	20
Chapter	3	Soldiers	24
Chapter	4	Refugee	27
Chapter	5	Hope and Despair	33
Chapter	6	Called by God	40
Chapter	7	Preparing to Serve God	47
Chapter	8	Where is Ibillin?	52
Chapter	9	Seeking Dignity and Hope	57
Chapter	10	Impossible Dreams?	61
Chapter	11	Life at Mar Elias	72
Chapter	12	Hope for the Future	77

Resources:

A Note to Parents and Teachers	82
Questions to Think about and Discuss	83
Words and facts	88
Archbishop Elias Chacour – Awards and Accomplishments	97
Pilgrims of Ibillin	99

Blessed are the Peacemakers

Foreword

When I read the book, *Blessed Are The Peacemakers,* I was very impressed with the analysis of my own story. As the Archbishop of Galilee of the Melkite Christian Community, the largest Christian community in Israel/Palestine, I want to stress the importance of witnessing for Christ, his resurrection and mainly for his presence among us today. This story illustrates very much in depth this goal.

I would like to thank Patricia Griggs for her work because it is a ministry to the young people to teach them that goodness is stronger than evil and they can make an impact and bring about change if they take seriously their faith, and if they are educated to choose between good and good, and not between good and bad. We need to teach our children that evil is not a choice. Evil is the absence of choice. Sin is no choice. It is the absence of hope.

It is important to give hope to young people and to nurture in them, not only in the abstract love of God, but the translation of that love for our neighbor, our brother, our sister, and all human beings. They need to see in the face of our neighbors the beauty of God's creation. Sometimes we need to close our physical eyes and open the eyes of the mind, spirit, and soul to see that God is present in us and in others. We have two places where we can see God very clearly. If we close our eyes and go in depth into our own soul we remember we are created in the image and likeness of God. Our place is to open our eyes and look left and right and say to ourselves, "I am seeing what God has created, most beautiful."

The questions at the end of the book for each chapter are important. They stimulate young people not only to read the story, but also to write in their mind the story they want to be in the future.

I hope the reader of this book will realize that what is written here is the true story. It is a true story of a boy, of a man who lives in Galilee. It is the same Galilee where Jesus Christ lived his life and where he watched everything that was there and used it to teach about God, and humanity.

I hope the reader will also become aware that there are Palestinian Christians who consider themselves to be the descendants of the first apostles, the first Christian community. That community met the first time in the Upper Room and received the Holy Spirit. Because of that they cleansed their minds of all preconceived ideas and became aware of the importance of the man, Jesus the Christ, with whom they were living. He had been crucified and was raised and gave them the gift of the Holy Spirit. They became his witnesses.

And that is exactly what we Palestinian Christians have been doing for centuries and centuries and especially the plight of the Palestinians since 1948. We were expected to react violently with everything that surrounded us, but we did not do so. We reacted with good for evil, with forgiveness for insults. We welcomed our Jewish brothers and sisters. Our deepest wish is that everyone understands no matter what they do to us we cannot hate them, and never hate them, because they are part of this most beautiful creation of God.

Archbishop Elias Chacour

Introduction

Archbishop Elias Chacour is an Arab Christian who grew up during the time of the Zionist take over of Palestine and the establishment of the State of Israel. All his life he has seen discrimination, conflict, war, and the suffering of both Palestinians and Israelis. Instead of growing up bitter and full of hatred because of what happened to him and his family, he grew up to be a priest and is known world wide as a peacemaker. This book was written to help the reader capture a glimpse into his world and understand how he has had the courage and conviction to seek peaceful solutions to conflict, and to forgive those who persecute him and others.

I met Archbishop Chacour (Abuna) in 1996 when my husband and I took a group of teenagers from our church on a pilgrimage and work camp to Israel. We spent one of our weeks in the Arab village of Ibillin in Israel working at the Mar Elias Educational Institutions (MEEI) campus. Father Chacour would work alongside us at the work sites, gardening, painting, or moving floor tiles.

Sometimes he would disappear for a while in the afternoon. When we saw him again at dinner we would ask, "Where did you go Abuna?" Usually he would tell us about his meeting with an ambassador, a statesman, or a group from another country visiting the campus. Once we learned that he had gone to give one of his regular addresses on Israeli TV. We began to understand that this man was doing more than building schools. He was influencing leaders of countries all over the world. As a result of his peacemaking efforts he has been nominated for the Nobel Peace Prize three times.

At night after dinner Abuna would invite us to sit in his garden or on the roof of his home and listen to him tell stories. He would weave biblical stories with current events and the holy sites we had visited that afternoon. It seemed like he had come that day from visiting with Jesus on the hillside. Bible stories came alive for us. We could see that this man's courage to be a peacemaker came from his solid grounding in the teachings of Jesus and the presence of

Jesus in his life. Listening to Abuna changed the lives of many of our youth and adults.

Since that time my husband and I have been back to MEEI a number of times building relationships with the students, faculty and Abuna. I have heard his stories as well as those of other Palestinians and Israelis as they told of their experiences during the establishment of the State of Israel. I have used Father Chacour's voice when writing the stories so they would appear as he has told them to me.

My encounters with the Christians, Muslims and Jews of the Holy Land have convinced me of the importance of sharing Elias Chacour's story. This book was written to help young people see how their faith can change their lives and the lives of those around them when they dedicate themselves to be faithful followers of Jesus as peacemakers.

While traveling in Palestine and Israel and staying at the schools in Ibillin we met wonderful people of all faiths who believe in peace. We have come to understand that it is dangerous to generalize when talking about any one religious group. In each group there are people who have many different ideas about how peace should be achieved.

The tragedy of wars and conflicts in the Middle East continue to this day. By learning how to bring about justice and peace in our own family and community we can learn to be peacemakers in the larger society of the world. The purpose of the book is not only to tell the story of a remarkable man, but also to help the reader realize he or she can be empowered by faith in God and Jesus to be a peacemaker. May God bless you on your journey of faith and peacemaking.

Patricia R. Griggs

Greetings

Hello! My name is Elias Chacour. As a boy I lived in the little village of Biram, located on the northern border of what was Palestine and is now the State of Israel.

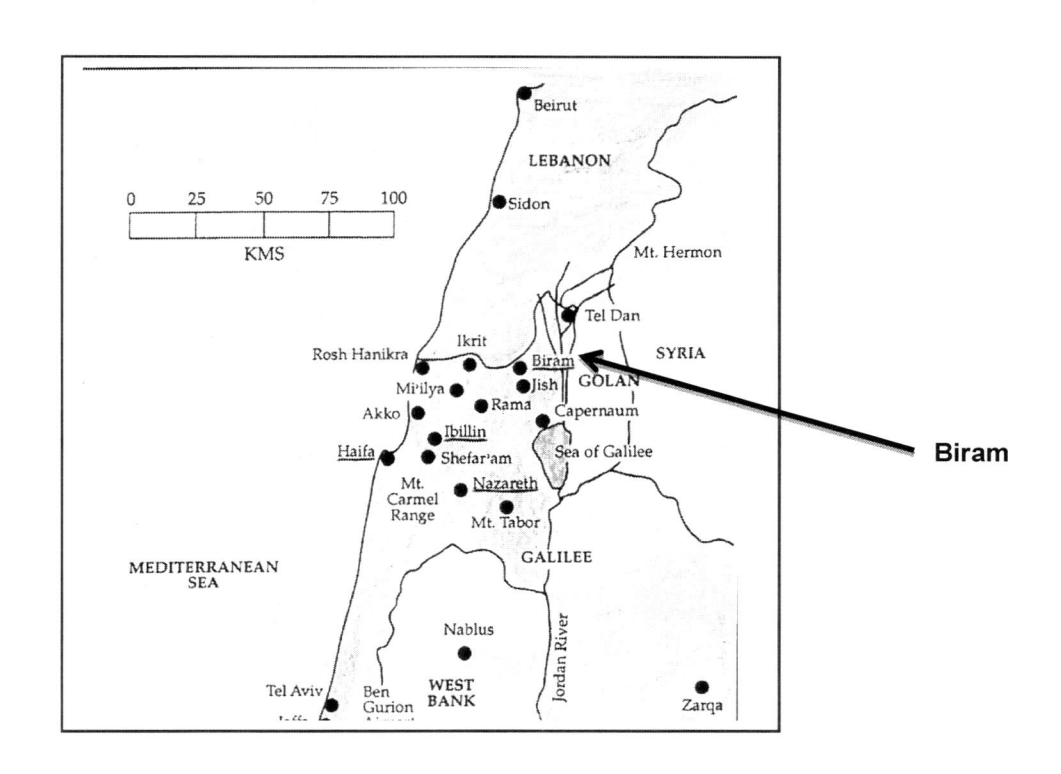

Israel/ Palestine

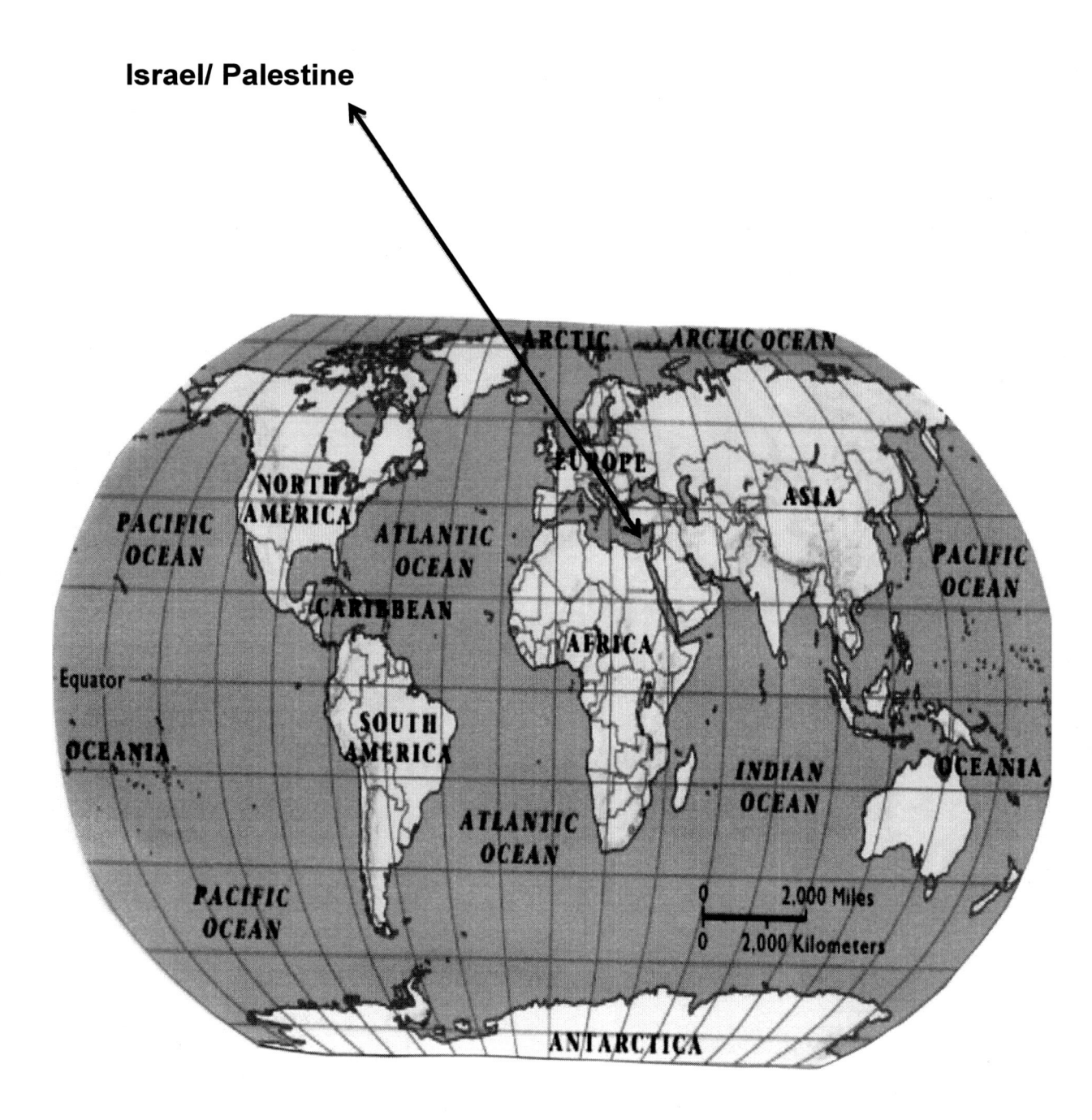

I have lived all my life in the land in which Jesus was born. I am a Christian who believes strongly in the teachings of Jesus. I have devoted my life to following his teachings. Following the teachings of Jesus has led me to be a peacemaker.

I am an Arab Palestinian Christian and a citizen of the State of Israel. Many people think that if you live in Israel you are Jewish. That is not true. Jewish people do live in Israel, but so do Christians, Druze and Muslims. Many people think all Arabs are Muslims. They are not. There are also Arab Christians.

If these words: Arab, Palestinian, Christian and Israeli are not familiar to you, look in the back of this book and you will find definitions of these and many other words that you will find in my story.

I would like to tell you my story to help you understand how my Christian faith has given me:
- *Strength* to face many hard times,
- *Courage* to stand up for those who are oppressed, and
- *Wisdom* that has helped me become a peacemaker.

Perhaps after reading my story you will begin to understand how your Christian faith can give you compassion and courage to be a peacemaker. You can start now, no matter how old you are or where you live.

Chapter 1

My Home — Biram
1947

To understand my story, you need to know something about my family and what my village of Biram was like when I was a child. I would like you to come with me for a walk through my village as I share my memories.

The village was located at the top of a hill and my house was on the edge of the village with a view of the valley and my father's beautiful orchards. We will start our visit to the village at my house.

My house and all the buildings are built from the large stones found in the fields around the village. The men of the village built everything with their bare hands. They carried the stones from the fields, shaped them and fit them together to make the walls of the buildings. Our house had a large room with a well in the corner and a place for a cooking fire that mother would use in the winter when we could not cook outside. There was a loft for sleeping and a small room off the big room where we kept our animals. We also had a room to keep the food for the animals. The roof of the house was flat so we could go up there to sleep on hot summer nights. In the front of the house we had a place to cook and an oven made of stone where mother baked bread and other good food.

There are six children in my family. I have four brothers and one sister. My brothers are (from oldest to youngest): Rudah, Chacour, Musah, and Atallah. (Yes, one of my brothers has as his first and last name, Chacour). My sister is Wardi and then there is me - Elias. I am the youngest in my family. My mother's name is Katoub and father is Michael.

Our days were very simple. Mother would get up early in the morning and start cooking and baking. After seeing all the children off to school she would spend the day doing chores and visiting with her friends in the village. Our family of six children was not unusual. Some families had as many as fifteen or more children. Voices of children and adults and laughter filled the air. So did the smells of good things cooking. Today, whenever I smell bread baking I can close my eyes and see myself back in our home in Biram and remember the wonderful taste of mother's bread as she fed it to us warm from the oven.

After school we all had chores to do. My sister Wardi's job was to feed sticks to the cooking fire. My brothers hauled wood and water. I often helped haul water but I tried to get out of doing chores. We all were supposed to help father in the orchards. Each day father worked in the orchard or went to another village to trade.

From our house we could see down into the valley where my father's orchards stretched out to the hills. The Chacour family tended those orchards longer than anyone can remember. Just a little way down the hill from my house I had a favorite fig tree at the edge of the orchard. I would go there and climb up to the top of the tree to escape doing chores, or to look over the valley to the far away hills of the Galilee. I wondered what it would be like to walk the hills where Jesus walked. Maybe Jesus walked through our valley and ate fruit from the trees.

Biram is an old Christian village where the same families have lived for generations. I have heard my father and my grandparents tell me stories about their grandfathers, great grandfathers and their fathers before them who lived here. It was the same for the other families of Biram, and because we were a small village, living here was like living in a great big family. Everyone knew everyone else and their histories.

Ours was a peaceful village where I felt safe and secure. Some might say that we were a poor village. We did not have electricity, running water, a library or a movie theater or lots of stores. Life was very simple in Biram, but we were very happy.

From our house we would walk down the path between other houses around the chickens and goats to the church and school.

Notre Dame Church in Biram

There were no roads, just paths between the houses.

The whole village worshiped in our church and this is where I was baptized. I remember that day well. I was four years old and my brother Atallah was six. Atallah went first to be baptized. Our priest, Abu Eed, anointed him with oil and then immersed him in water. I wanted to be baptized, but I did not want to take my clothes off. So when it was my turn and Abu Eed reached for me I turned and ran. I ran until I found a woodpile and hid until my mother talked me into coming out later in the morning. Everyone teased me. They said I was half Christian because I did not finish my baptism. The next year I agreed to being baptized if I could do it without taking off my clothes!

The church   The Parish House

Right next to the church was our school. We called it the Parish House. Education was highly valued because most of the adults in Biram had not had the opportunity to go to school to learn to read and write. They made the education of their children a top priority.

Each morning before leaving for school Mother would stop preparing the bread dough and give us an inspection. She would look to be sure our clothes were clean and neat, our faces washed and our hair combed. With her words of encouragement we would run out the door, eager to get school. I loved school from the first day.

Cousins and friends would join us as we ran to the courtyard that was between the church and the Parish House. We were trying to get there before the huge bronze bell on top of the church began to ring. The first four grades, which included my class, met in the Parish House. The walls were thick and squat with huge open windows through which we could see the valley.

Abu 'Eed was our teacher as well as our priest. He was very kind and the only priest in our village. He taught us math, spelling, reading, geography and the Bible.

Going to school was like discovering a new world. It was a place of new and wonderful ideas. The more Abu Eed told us about the world outside our village, the more I wanted to learn and the more I wanted to see the world. Everything about school excited me. We did not have markers or white boards, lots of books or art supplies like schools do today, but we had a wonderful skilled teacher and a hunger for learning.

Leaving the church and school and continuing on the path down the hill, we come to the village square. This was where the men of the village gathered to exchange news or trade with people from other villages. They came to trade their produce or things they made in their village for our produce and products. It was always a busy place and a place where children were not allowed to play.

We played around our houses or out in the fields or down by the stream. Some of my best memories are of the games we played after school. We never ran out of ideas of things to do.

In the springtime when the ground was still damp, we gathered little sticks and threw them to try and get them to stand up in the soft ground. The object was to knock down each other's sticks and when you did you got to take the stick you knocked down. The winner was the one who had the most sticks at the end of the game.

Sometimes we would spread sticky goo on sticks and put them in the trees. Birds would get stuck in the goo and we could catch them, take them home, and fix them for dinner.

Sometimes we would go fishing. We would catch the fish with our hands and put them in a bucket of water to take home and put in cisterns to grow. They would eat the insects and when they were big enough we would catch them again and cook them for dinner.

One of my favorite games was to have poetry competitions to find out who knew the most poems. We did not just recite them. We played a game by taking the last letter of the last word of the poem one person would recite and making it the first letter of the first word with which the next person would start his or her poem.

Our games were very simple. There were no computers or the interesting toys and games boys and girls enjoy today. But, we had fun.

From the village square you could walk to a road that goes past our village to the village of Gish. The road goes past Gish to the Mount of the Beatitudes and the Sea of Galilee's northern shore. I often wondered what it would be like to follow that road and see what the world was like outside my village.

After school our lessons continued at home. In the evening mother and father taught us about our family history, our culture and faith. Every afternoon, when I was not helping in the fields, I would find mother. I loved to snuggle on her lap and listen to her tell me stories from the Bible. She had a wonderful memory. She could not read, but after hearing a story a couple of times she could remember it. She told the stories so well I could picture the people and places in my mind. She told me Old Testament stories about David, Solomon, Abraham, Sarah and others. But, as wonderful as these stories were, the stories about Jesus were my favorite.

Mother told me that Jesus might have walked the dusty roads into our own village. I learned that Jesus had come to Galilee, to our hills and our people. Did he visit our village after his temptation in the wilderness (Mt 4:1-11)? I wonder if Jesus may have given someone from the Chacour family bread to eat (Mt. 14.13-21). Maybe a Chacour boy or girl felt Jesus fingertips when Jesus blessed the little children (Mt. 19.13-15), or watched as Jesus healed the sick and the blind (Mt. 20.29 – 34). These wonders were real to me, for they had occurred on streets and in homes like those I saw every day.

For example, I understood the story of the paralyzed man being lowered through the roof so Jesus could heal him (Mk 2.1-12) because Jesus would have been seated inside a simple Galilean home just like ours.

Well – (Cistern)   Storage room for animal feed

This shows the inside of the large main room of Elias' aunt's house after it was destroyed. A door would have been in the arch instead of the rocks blocking the arch in this picture.

The large main room is where guests were welcomed. Jesus, as an honored guest, would have been seated against the rear wall between the well and the storage room. The house had a stone roof, but the storage room roof had wooden tiles that were easily removed so the feed for the animals could be pitched in from the outside. The men in the Bible story could easily have removed the roof tiles of the storage room and lowered their paralyzed friend right down into the doorway by Jesus' feet.

My brothers and I used to like to climb on the roof and jump down into the piles of hay. This did not please our mother.

I was reminded of Bible stories every time I heard the jingle of mother's necklace. Father had given her a necklace decorated with fish and doves on a simple chain that jingled when she walked. The fish represented Peter's fish in the nearby Sea of Galilee, (Mark 1.16-18, Luke 5.1-11) and the doves represented the Holy Spirit. They reminded us that the spirit had lighted upon Jesus at his baptism in the Jordan River (Matthew 3.16-17). She loved that necklace and wore it always.

While Mother told me Bible stories our father taught us history. He wanted to be sure his children knew their treasured Christian heritage that goes back to the first century. Night after night, father would gather all of us outside under the stars or inside around a fire to tell us stories. He wanted us to always remember two things.

1. We should love and respect our Galilean soil. Our family had tilled this land and worshipped here longer than anyone could remember.

2. We inhabited Palestine, with the Jews as our neighbors, and suffered with them under the rule of foreign powers throughout our history. We learned to share the simple elements of human existence: faith, reverence for life, and hospitality even when ruled by the Romans, Persians, Crusaders and Turks. Father said, "Faith, reverence for life and hospitality, were the things that caused people to live happily together".

Father taught us something even more valuable than our colorful history. He taught us by the way he lived how to live as a Christian.

My understanding of who Jesus was, most likely came from watching and listening to my other hero, my father.

Father was a calm, peaceful man. He would discipline us in a way that was not harsh but made us want to do the right thing. His faith made him a man of peace. We felt safe and peaceful when we were with him.

> His faith made him a man of peace.

Chapter 2

Trouble

One day I was up in my favorite tree again when I heard Atallah calling me.

"Here I am Atallah. Up here!" I called. "Come down. I have something really exciting to tell you," he replied. I could tell by the tone of his voice this was serious, so I swung from branch to branch until I was low enough to jump to the ground.

"All right. Here I am. What is so important?" I asked him.

Atallah said, "There is going to be a celebration. Something big is happening in the village. I don't know what, but father has gone to trade for a lamb!"
Before I could ask any questions Atallah ran to help mother and others clear away rocks in the garden plot. I ran to the village square. I should have gone with Atallah to help with the rocks. Clearing rocks was a hard job. When the rocks were very large, father would lay down on his back with his feet against the rock. Then he would push with all his strength to move it. I was too small to do that, but I could help with the smaller rocks.

I had to find out what was happening. Did everyone know but me? This had to be something big because having meat meant this would be a very special occasion. Usually we only had meat a few times a year and lamb was saved for our Easter celebration.

I knew the men of the village would be gathered in the village square and father might be there. I wanted to find him and find out exactly what was happening.

I did not see father when I reached the village square. I knew I was not supposed to be there and tried to keep from being seen, but one of the men saw me and wanted to know why I was there. I tried to act grown up and politely asked where I could find him. "He went trading today. I don't know where. Maybe he went to the Jewish village," replied the man. This was probably true. There was a lot of trading between their village and ours.

Thinking that father might be on his way home, I ran to look down the road. It was empty. I decided to return home and wait for father. When I saw mother sitting by the cooking fire I asked her what was happening in Biram. "Everyone knows but me," I said. She answered, "Wait for your father to come home. He wants to tell you himself. While you are waiting, go help your brother bring some water."

By the time Father arrived home with a lamb I was so full of questions I thought I would burst, but knew I had to wait until father had something to eat before I asked them. Just when I thought I could wait no longer, father called us to come and sit with him.

"I have something important to tell you," he said. He looked so sad I began to worry. Then he told us about a man named Hitler and how he led his army to find and kill Jewish people in Europe. We did not understand. Why would someone do that? Father told us that the only reason was because they were Jews. This did not make sense to me.

I asked, "Father what has this to do with Biram?" He explained that Hitler was dead now. The Jews who fled their homes in Europe no longer had homes to return to. They were looking for places to live. Many of them decided to come to Palestine to look for a home.

What father told us next caused us to become very worried. He said, "In a few days Jewish soldiers will be traveling through Biram. They are called *Zionists*. A few will stay in each home, including ours. They will stay maybe a week. Then they will move on. They are not coming to hurt us. You have no reason to be afraid. We must be especially kind and make them feel at home."

"That's why I traded for the lamb. We are going to prepare a feast. This year we will celebrate the Resurrection (Easter) early because our Jewish brothers and sisters who were threatened with death are alive."

We excitedly started asking father questions: "If the soldiers stay at our house, were will we sleep?" "If they are soldiers, will they have guns?" "How many are coming?"

Father told us we would sleep on the roof. We loved sleeping on the roof and looking at the sparkling stars in the dark night sky. We often slept there in the summer when it was hot. This time of year it would be cool. We would take blankets and it would be fun.

> Many houses in Israel have a flat roof. Inside the house is a sleeping loft with a door to the outside where you climb up the stairs to the roof.
>
> Stairs

He told us the soldiers would have guns, but they were not coming to harm us. They were just looking over the land to find good places where the Jewish people who were coming to Palestine could live. They would only stay with us a few days.

Father prayed: "God in heaven, help us to show love to our Jewish brothers and sisters. Help us to show them peace to quiet their troubled hearts. Amen"

I remember that after dinner we children talked about the soldiers and their visit. Rudah was especially worried about soldiers coming with guns even though father assured us that we should not be afraid. He said, "We don't have any guns except the old rusty one we use to scare wolves that come and try to steal animals from the village flock. What if the soldiers are not as friendly as father says they are?"

A few days later Rudah tried to sneak the old gun into the house. Father caught him and it was the only time I remember father showing real anger. He sternly said "Get that gun out of here! I won't have it in my house." We all froze and did not dare speak.

Father reached for the gun, and taking it away from Rudah said, in a calmer voice, "We never use violence to solve a problem. Never!" Rudah was very frightened and the rest of us did not understand why father would tell us not to use violence if we were in danger of being hurt.

Father must have known our concern because he told us, "This is not the first time the Jews have been rejected, hunted and killed. What they experienced in Europe was the worst time ever. After centuries of being treated so badly they have come to live in fear. Sometimes when people are afraid they carry guns."

Rudah was not satisfied. He kept asking questions wanting to be assured that we would be safe. At last father said something I never have forgotten. He said, "The Jews and Palestinians are family. We share the same father, Abraham, and the same God. We must never forget that we are blood brothers."

The time was soon coming when I would have little else to hold onto but my memories of the lessons my father and mother taught me, and the faith in God that they showed me.

> **"The Jews and Palestinians are family. We share the same father, Abraham, and the same God."**

Chapter 3

Soldiers

Soldiers are still seen in the streets of the occupied territories of Palestine

One morning several weeks later we heard the loud roaring of motors. Trucks and jeeps were driving to our village. My brothers and I ran from the house to watch as the soldiers got out of the vehicles and walked into the village. In little groups the soldiers went to each house including ours.

We were afraid, but Father was friendly toward them and welcomed them. We noticed right away that the Zionist soldiers were not at all like our friendly Jewish neighbors who visited with father and had coffee with him in the yard.

We all gathered to have the feast that mother and father had prepared. The food smelled wonderful. But instead of a happy celebration, the soldiers were quiet and unfriendly. Usually our celebrations were full of laughter and storytelling, but not this time.

The guns were a sign of power and the families of Biram had no such power. When we went to bed that first night it was hard to sleep. I couldn't stop thinking about the soldiers and their guns in the house below us. The next day we went to school and the soldiers were there with their guns. They were everywhere in the village. The village was no longer full of laughter and fun.

The soldiers had been with us for about a week and everyone was expecting them to leave soon. One day the military commander called the men of the village together. Instead of announcing that they were leaving, the commander said that Biram was in serious danger and to be safe we should leave the village. He told us we should move into the hills for a few days until the danger passed.

The families left the village and went into the Olive groves and the hills.

Some men from other villages told us there had been fighting in Jerusalem. So the men of Biram decided it would be best to keep their families safely out of the way if fighting was coming to Biram. The commander urged them to leave as soon as possible.

When work among the flocks and fields took us away from the shelter of our house we often slept on the ground. So leaving our homes for a couple of days and sleeping in the orchard was something we were used to. In fact, for us children this seemed like a fun adventure at first.

Mother and Father told us to hurry. We were to leave behind everything but the heavy clothes we were wearing. I was permitted to bring a blanket with me. Father locked the door and handed the key to one of our soldier-guests to take care of until we returned.

It felt strange to see everyone leaving the village together. The few people who were talking did so in quiet voices. Although we children saw this as an adventure, we knew the adults were worried and this kept us quieter than usual. It felt like a sad parade. We all headed to the olive groves. Each family found a spot and made a place to stay until the soldiers told us it was safe to return home. We did not expect to be there for more than a couple of days.

From the orchards the men could look up the hill and see the village. They watched to see what was happening. We wondered if other soldiers would come and the fighting would start. I heard the men talking. They wondered how long we would have to stay here, and about the fighting, and what was happening in the rest of the Galilee. As time went on they were beginning to wonder if they had made a mistake by following the soldiers' orders to leave. But, what else could they do? The soldiers had guns.

After a few days everyone was very uncomfortable. It was hard for the older people to sleep on the ground for more than a few nights. The weather did not help. It was hot during the day and cold at night. Everyone was thankful I had brought my blanket. All six of us children tried to squeeze under it while mother and father huddled together uncomfortably on the ground. Then it rained. The ground became muddy. People were getting soaked and cold.

Father had an idea. There was a grotto (cave) at the edge of the orchard. He took us there to get out of the rain and wind. The grotto was not very big but we squeezed in. It smelled damp and there was moss on the walls, but at least we were warmer and protected.

Everyone continued to camp. The men and older boys hunted for food, and brought water to drink from the springs. Everyone watched the village. We saw jeeps and trucks coming and going, but there was no fighting.

Chapter 4

Refugees

The leaders of the village grew more and more concerned. They decided to go to Biram and talk to the military commander to find out how much longer we had to wait before returning home. When they reached Biram they were shocked to see that the homes had been broken into. Furniture and belongings were gone or smashed and scattered on the floor.

Our men were angry. "Where is your commanding officer?" they asked. The soldiers held their guns across their chest and asked, "What are you doing here? You have no business here. You don't belong here. Leave!" Our men looked at the soldiers with shock and disbelief. "Don't belong here? This is our village. Our homes are here. We were told to leave to be safe from the fighting and we could come back in a few days." The soldier replied, "I don't know what you are talking about. This village is ours. Go back where you came from. We were told to protect this village."

Our men could not believe what they were hearing. They started to protest, but the soldiers had guns and when they pointed them at the men and in angry voices told them to leave, they did so.

None of us could believe what had happened. We had trusted these soldiers. Pain was on every face. Such behavior was beyond our understanding. What were we going to do now? We did not have any way of fighting with these soldiers. No one could think of a way to get our village back.

Someone suggested that we climb the next hill to Gish, (Jish) our nearest neighboring village. The people who lived there were Christians. Surely they would help us until we could straighten things out.

As we approached Gish we began to worry. There were no shepherds in the open fields around the village. No children were playing in the soccer lot. In fact there was no one around. Where was everyone? The village was silent.

Finally we found a handful of elderly people who told us they were the only ones in the village. Soldiers had come and with guns ordered everyone to leave. People had scattered. Some went across the border to Lebanon. Others ran into the hills.

We told them what had happened to us and asked if we could find shelter in Gish. They were glad to have us join them in the village. Everyone started looking for an empty house in which to stay. We discovered that the soldiers had treated these houses the same way they had in Biram. Inside the houses furniture had been removed or destroyed.

Finding a place to stay was not easy. Gish was a smaller village than Biram so there were fewer houses. Sometimes two families were cramped into a single room. Father found a one-room house for us. It was empty except for a few broken chairs.

This is the home where the Chacour family stayed in Gish.

The men wondered if it would be safe to go to some of the nearby villages and find out what was happening in the rest of the Galilee. Before they did, some people came to us from other villages and told us that soldiers were driving the people from their villages all over Galilee. Would the soldiers come back and make us leave Gish? If they did, where would we go? We lived in fear. Mother and father tried to assure us that we were safe, but we did not feel safe any more.

As people from other villages came through Gish we began to hear news about what was going on in the world. We heard the terrible news that the future of our land was being determined by other powerful nations. The Zionists wanted to establish a national homeland that they would name "The State of Israel". The land they wanted was where we lived — Palestine. No one could stop them from taking over our land. They claimed this was the land God promised to Moses (Deut. 1. 6-8) and so it was their land. The situation came before the United Nations. We prayed the rumors we heard were not true. The rumors were that Palestine was going to be divided between the Zionists and the Palestinians.

The summer of 1949 passed. Month after month we lived in our cramped quarters and prayed for the news that we could return to our homes in Biram.

In November we learned that the rumors were true. Over half of Palestine was to be given to the Zionists. Less than half would be for Palestinians. Many Palestinians who had not been driven from their villages were being told to hand over their homes and farmlands even though the land had been in their families for generations. They were being forced to become refugees. There was nothing fair about this, but it seemed there was nothing the Palestinians could do.

The Jews, who were our neighbors and friends and shared our customs, ached for us. They could not understand or accept what was happening, but they too were powerless to help.

Father believed that God had promised to feed and protect us. He prayed for those who had made themselves our enemies. I listened to him pray: "Forgive them God. Heal their pain. Remove their bitterness. Let us show them your peace."

We had been refugees in Gish for more than two years. One night the soldiers came to the village and we heard a voice over a loudspeaker commanding that all the men and older boys leave their homes and come out to the street. Soldiers were hurrying the men and older boys at gunpoint into open-backed trucks. The women and children were crying and calling to their husbands and sons. I was still too young for the soldiers to take me. The tailgates slammed shut and the trucks rolled away into the night with my father, my brothers, and the other men of the village. Those horrible hours turned into days. Mother's strength and inner peace came from prayer. She softly prayed.

> "Lord, only you know where Michael and the boys are this night. Will you watch over them for us and keep them safe? We place them in your care. Allow us to be your servants here in Gish. Use our lips, hands and feet to comfort the suffering and bring the peace of your Spirit. Amen"

Time passed. One day I climbed alone to the top of a hill and sat beneath an olive tree. Almost without thinking I began to pour out my heart to God in prayer. "God, can't you make all this trouble go away? What do you want us to do? Mother prays for us to be your lips and hands and feet, She wants peace again. Do you want us to be your lips, hands and feet? If so, you can use mine."

> **"Do you want us to be your lips, hands and feet?**
>
> **If so, you can use mine."**

This was one of the most important prayers of my life. It was the first small step on the long journey of becoming a peacemaker.

Weeks and weeks passed and still we had no word about the men who had been taken from us. Were they alive? Were they hurt? Where were they? What did the soldiers do to them? Many nights I cried myself to sleep as I worried about and missed my father and brothers.

One night after mother had locked the door for the night we heard a noise. Mother, Wardi, Atallah and I sat up, listening. The bolt rattled in its lock. Someone was trying to open the door. Fear ran down my spine. Were the soldiers back? A muffled voice from outside hissed, "Let us in. Quickly." Fear gripped all of us. Were the soldiers trying to trick us into opening the door?

Mother stood frozen by the door and said, "Who is it?" The voice said in a loud whisper, "Let us in. Hurry…" "Go away," Mother called. She was next to tears. "It is Michael. Let us in. We are home." Mother shrieked, "Michael!"

We all ran to the door. Mother slammed back the bolt and threw open the heavy door. Four men pushed inside. At first I did not recognize them. They looked like strangers. They were thin. Their beards were uncut. Their clothes were dirty and ragged. Mother knew them right away. She hugged and kissed them, and wept for joy. I threw my arms around Father's waist and a wave of relief spread through my body.

We sat up most of the night listening to father tell us about their journey. The soldiers had taken them through the hill country that rose up to Jerusalem. The trucks pulled off the road near the town of Nablus on the border between the new state of Israel and the Kingdom of Jordan and let everyone out. Men ran in all directions as the soldiers fired their guns above their heads. They wanted to drive everyone across the border and out of Israel. Father and my brothers ran until they were out of range of the bullets. They looked for a road that would take them north and started walking, always watching for soldiers. They stopped at some of the towns on the way asking for shelter and food, but were turned away. People were afraid to help them. They traveled for weeks sleeping in abandoned animal shelters in the hills or sleeping in the dirt and grass. When they reached the fields outside Gish, they waited until dark in case soldiers were guarding the village. Then, they crept though the streets to the house. Mother was very embarrassed when father teased her about refusing to open the door to her own husband.

In the coming months a few more men returned, but many did not. We never found out what happened to them. I lived in fear that the soldiers would surprise us and take the men away again. They never did.

In the closing months of 1950, we received the news we had all been waiting for. A letter arrived from the Supreme Court of Israel that said we could return to Biram! We had not known such joy in years. Everyone made plans for the move home. But when we got to Biram the commanding officer shook his head and said, "This letter means nothing to us. The village is ours. You have no right to be here."

Blessed are the Peacemakers

A map of Biram plus two documents from the Israeli Supreme Court sent to the families of Biram.

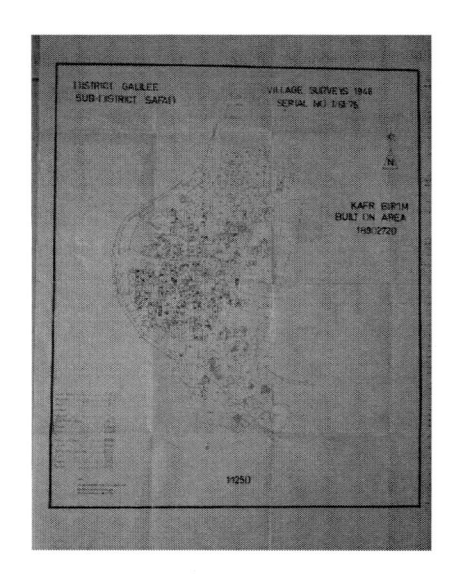

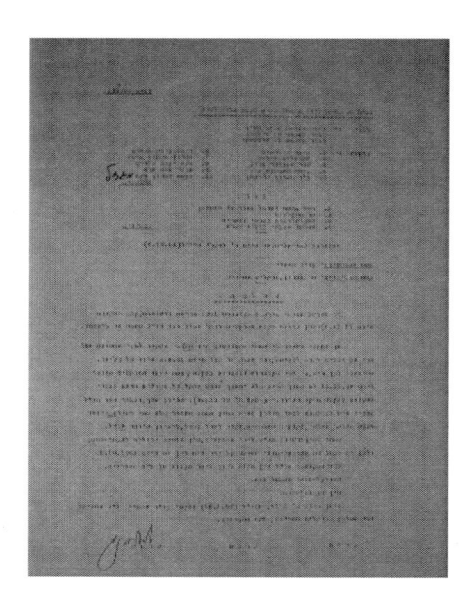

Chapter 5

Hope and Despair
1951

We looked forward to visits by our Bishop. He faithfully visited all the villages and refugees every month. We depended on him to bring us food, clothing, and medical supplies. One day my farther said to the Bishop, "My youngest son Elias is a good student. I want to send him to a good school. Please, can you help me?"

The Bishop told him about an orphanage near the Bishop's home in Haifa where I could receive a good education. The Bishop said that even though I was not an orphan, he would see that I was accepted there. He promised to see to my education personally.

Father was very grateful and hurried to tell mother of this wonderful plan. Mother was not enthused. It was very hard for her to consider sending her youngest child so far from home. Haifa was on the coast, many miles from Gish. Father assured her that the Bishop would care for me. After some time to think about it she agreed.

Father told me about his conversation with the Bishop and said that in a few days they would go with me on the bus to Haifa. Then he told me something I have never forgotten. He said, "You are going to study with the Bishop. This is a wonderful opportunity for you, Elias. You will never have a chance for an education here in Gish. I want you to understand that you are not being sent away to be spoiled by privilege. Learn all you can from the Bishop. If you become a true man of God you will know how to reconcile enemies and how to turn hatred into peace. Only a true servant of God can do that."

Elias Chacour at 12 years old when he left home to go to Haifa to school.

*"If you become a true man of God,
you will know how to reconcile enemies
and turn hatred into peace.
Only a true servant of God can do that."*

The morning I was to leave I woke to the sound of mother's necklace as it jingled while she packed my things. All of a sudden I did not feel at all adventurous. A big lump formed in my throat and my stomach ached. I could hardly eat my breakfast I was so excited. At the same time I was frightened to leave home and all that was familiar to me.

The whole family walked with me to the bus stop. When the bus arrived my bag was loaded and mother, father, and I climbed aboard. I looked out the back window of the bus at my brothers and Wardi. Suddenly I realized I did not know when I would see them again. It was an awful feeling. I felt the excitement of leaving my home and seeing at last what was beyond my valley. At the same time I almost felt sick leaving my family.

Haifa was very different than what I was used to. Instead of the hills, orchards and our small village, I found myself surrounded by buildings. There were people and cars everywhere. It was noisy. I became conscious of how I was dressed. All I had were old clothes chosen from the piles of clothes the Bishop had brought to the village on one of his visits. Everyone I saw was in beautiful clothes. For the first time I was aware that as a refugee, I was different.

Father led us through the busy streets. Sometimes I could see down the hill to the beautiful Mediterranean Sea. I had never seen so much water.

Finally we reached the Bishop's orphanage. A young woman welcomed us warmly. The Bishop introduced us to a couple of other women from France and Belgium. They lived with the orphans as their way of serving the church.

This is the way the building looks today. It is no longer an orphanage.

Much too soon, mother and father were hugging me and saying goodbye. I felt so alone when they were gone. Would I ever return home? When would I see my family again? If I wanted to leave, could I find my way home?

The young woman tried to comfort me. I think she knew how I was feeling because she gently laid an arm across my slumping shoulder as I stared at the empty street. "Come, Elias," she said tenderly. "I want you to come and meet the other orphans."

I was used to quiet open spaces. Here it was noisy and full of concrete. I said the words over and over from the New Testament that Mother often quoted: "I am with you always." (Matt. 28.20) The words comforted me, but, I was lonely.

After a while the routine of study, play and sleep filled my days. Although I loved to study, I still missed the quiet of my home and having time to be alone. I longed for the days when I could go into the quiet hills of Galilee and feel the presence of Jesus. One evening I found the quiet I longed for. I was in the big common room where we could study and play. This night one of the housemothers came to tell us it was time for bed. I guess she saw how discouraged I looked because she said, "You are a good student Elias. I am sure you will be quiet and not disturb anyone if I allow you to stay here a little longer."

Staying up longer than the others began a routine. Each night, after the others left and I was alone, I would sit and write letters to Jesus. I told him my most secret thoughts. I told him how confused I was about what was happening in Israel/Palestine. I did not understand why good people like my father and mother had to suffer. I asked Jesus if it was God's plan that the non-violence my father insisted on was really the way to peace. I prayed that someone would help and the Court would order the military to allow my family and the other villagers to return to Biram. All I wanted was for our families to go home.

Before I knew it, it was Christmas. This was a happy time in the orphanage. We had a big Nativity celebration in the cathedral-like church with bells and the singing of carols. I remembered Christmas at home in Biram. Where and how was my family celebrating Christmas this year? As I sat in this beautiful church I felt a holiness and wonder that warmed me. In fact, being in church had come to feel like being at home to me. I loved it.

In January 1952 I was in worship in the chilliness of the old church when out of the corner of my eye I thought I saw my brother Rudah. It could not be. I could hardly wait for the service to be over so I could turn around and see if he was really there.

As soon as the service was over I stood up and turned around and sure enough, it was Rudah. I ran down the crowded aisle to him.

"Rudah!" I threw my arms around him. "I've missed you. I am so glad to see you. How long can you stay? Why are you here? How are Mother and Father?

When I looked up at my brothers' face I knew something was wrong. His face was solemn and serious. He looked like he might cry. I was suddenly frightened. Did something happen to mother and father?

We went outside and Rudah turned to me and said, "Mother and father sent me to tell you the news. They did not want you to hear it from someone else and worry about us." Fighting back tears he told me the horrible news. This is what he said:

> *"In early December, the Court granted us permission again to return to Biram. For the second time, the village elders marched across the hill from Gish to Biram. They showed the Zionist soldiers the letter from the government that said we could return to our village.*
>
> *We were surprised when they returned to us and told us that the commanding officer said the letter was fine. The soldiers would be out of the village by December twenty-fifth after which everyone could return.*
>
> *We were all so excited. What an incredible Christmas this was going to be. At long last, we would all be going home. Christmas Eve we gathered to sing and pray. We were filled with thanksgiving and joy.*
>
> *Early Christmas morning we gathered to start the march to Biram. As we walked we sang Christmas hymns. It had been four years since we had been forced and tricked out of our homes.*
>
> *When Biram came into sight we saw Zionists tanks, bulldozers and other military vehicles around Biram. We had been told we were supposed to return home Christmas day. We asked, 'Why were the soldiers still here?'*
>
> *Then a terrible thing happened. A soldier yelled something when he saw us and suddenly the air was filled with the sounds of cannons blasting our village. The soldiers opened fire on Biram. Tank shells shrieked into the village destroying our homes. Stones and dust were flying everywhere.*

Fires started and black smoke rose above the village like angry clouds. Shells hit the church and the bell tower fell. Airplanes came and started shelling the village. This lasted for maybe 5 minutes but it seemed like an hour. Just as suddenly as it started, it stopped.

We stood there stunned. The silence was broken with the sounds of crying and the terrified screams of the children. Mother and Father stood shaking, huddled together with us.

We all watched bulldozers drive through what was left of the village knocking down much of what had not already been blown apart.

Father, with his arms around us quietly said, 'Forgive them'. Then he led all of us back to Gish."

I was speechless. How could this be true? He told me that another village, Ikrit, had also been shelled at about the same time. I simply felt cold. Many years later I learned that over 450 villages had been destroyed and thousands of Palestinians became refugees.

When it was time for Rudah to leave I clung to him. I did not want to let go. That night I picked at my supper in silence. I could not get the picture of what happened out of my mind. The housemothers had heard the news from Rudah and realized I was too upset to expect me to do my schoolwork. They were extra kind to me that night.

That night when I was in the common room alone, I was frightened by my own thoughts. I did not know how to handle my anger. The destruction of our village was worse than anything I could imagine.

I felt like I had been beaten up, but worse. I could not even write in my journal I was so upset. Most of all I was ashamed to write down my feelings because they were so ugly. Eventually I calmed down enough to ask Jesus: "Will we ever have the peace we used to share with our Jewish neighbors?" I wondered if there was some way I could help my parents. I asked God, "Is there any way I can help my Palestinian people?"

I did not know what to do. I wanted to leave Haifa and return to my family and share their lives as refugees. It was going to be a hard life for them. Maybe if I were there I could help. But, I knew this is not what my father and mother wanted. I knew it was very important to them that I continue my studies. I knew I must stay. The Bishop and the orphanage would care for and instruct me. I would study hard and learn all I could. With all the people of Biram, I would continue to live the life of the homeless and the orphaned.

Chapter 6

Called by God
1953

I could not stop thinking about Biram and was discouraged, angry and sad most of the time. I longed to walk on the hills of the Galilee, or sit in my favorite tree. As much as I loved learning, I missed my home and my family.

I was given the gift of friendship by another boy my age, Faraj. He was the kind of person who always had an easy laugh and the ability to make those around him feel better about themselves. When I was around Faraj I was able to set some of my sadness aside and relax and enjoy myself. We were both thirteen. We became close friends.

A beach on the Mediterranean Sea

One day everyone from the orphanage went to the beach to swim in the nearby Mediterranean Sea. While the others were playing and splashing in the water I walked away from the crowd on the beach. I enjoyed being alone and the water had a calming effect on me. Faraj knew I liked to be alone, but he must have realized I was feeling sad because this day, he came to walk with me. As we walked along on the hot sand we talked about our families and wondered about what our future would be like now that there was a new government.

I asked Faraj, "What do you think will happen to us? What do you plan to do when we are through with our studies here? The university does not welcome Palestinians."

"I'm not sure," he said. As we continued to talk we realized that God had taken care of us so far by surrounding us with people who cared for us. We believed that God would continue to care for us. Faraj and I became very close friends, studying in the same classes and sharing late-night secrets when we ought to have been asleep.

In the fall of 1953 I enjoyed a rare visit to my family in Gish. I told them that the Bishop had talked about a new school in Nazareth for young men who were considering service to the Church. Father asked, "What do you want to do Elias?"

I was surprised that he asked me and did not just tell me what to do. It made me realize father thought I was old enough to make my own decisions. This was a big one and I had to give it more thought. The Bishop told us it would not be an easy life. He said serving the church would require obedience to God and to our superiors. Is this the kind of life I wanted?

When I returned to Haifa the Bishop asked Faraj and me if we had made a decision. Without hesitation we both replied that we did want to study in Nazareth. The kind Bishop smiled at us with his approval and joy at our answer.

When we arrived at St. Joseph's Minor Seminary in Nazareth in 1954, a young man called a Brother, wearing a grey robe, greeted us. After asking who we were he led Faraj and me into a dormitory. He told us we were expected at prayers soon and not to be late. We soon discovered that this place was very different than the homey orphanage we had left behind. The buildings were cold and there were no curtains on the windows or homey touches anywhere.

We put our things away and began to meet the other boys who had arrived before us. By the time we left for prayers we were talking and laughing together. The service had started by the time we got to the church. At the entrance one of the Brothers gave us a stern look to stop our great time and showed us into the sanctuary. Embarrassed, we slid quietly onto a bench near the back.

Up at the front of the sanctuary, a Brother was reading the Bible. His rich voice echoed through the silent church. I felt at home again. The hushed, worshipful atmosphere reminded me of the peace that I had felt in the hills of Biram. In a split second I was reliving those endless days when it seemed that I was actually walking with my childhood champion, Jesus. I felt a rush of joy stirring my spirit.

During the weeks to come I would look for a chance to slip away into the church where I felt close to the heart of God. Many times Faraj would join me. Once while we were alone in the church, Faraj looked at me and said, "You feel Jesus too, don't you?" I was surprised. How wonderful to share this closeness to Jesus with my good friend.

I loved the peacefulness that I felt when I was in the church so much that sometimes at night I felt a strong urge to go there to feel God's presence. One night I got up and dressed quietly. Being careful not to wake anyone, I made my way out of the room and slipped into the cool air of the night. I entered the church and sat on a bench in awe of the beauty of the sanctuary. As I sat there I recalled the words of many of my favorite passages of scripture that my mother taught me.

I found myself thinking about the Beatitudes (Mt 5.1-12). I was always puzzled by these words. I could not understand what was meant by "the meek inheriting the earth." The families of Biram had tried to live in peace but were kicked out of their homes and not allowed to return. They were persecuted. Are they blessed?

Blessed are the poor in spirit, for theirs is the kingdom of heaven.
Blessed are those who mourn, for they will be comforted.
Blessed are the meek, for they will inherit the earth.
Blessed are those who hunger and thirst for righteousness, for they will be filled.
Blessed are the merciful, for they will receive mercy.
Blessed are the pure in heart, for they will see God.
Blessed are the peacemakers, for they will be called children of God.
Blessed are those who are persecuted for righteousness' sake, for theirs is the kingdom of heaven.
Blessed are you when people revile you and persecute you and utter all kinds of evil against you falsely on my account.
Rejoice and be glad, for your reward is great in heaven, for in the same way they persecuted the prophets who were before you.

Matt. 5.3-12

I stayed in the sanctuary thinking and praying for so long I fell asleep.

The morning sunlight was streaming through the windows when I was shaken awake by one of the Brothers. He was not pleased with me. We were not supposed to leave the dormitory at night. He said that falling asleep praying and thinking was no excuse for breaking the rules. "We're going to the principal," he said.

I explained what had happened but the principal said, "I'm sorry Elias. You have broken the rules. You must be punished."

My punishment was 40 days of restriction. It was not the last time my independence or quick tongue would get me into trouble.

One day the Archbishop came to inspect our school. When he stood before us we were to stand up and bow to show our respect. The Archbishop would then call us by name and state the town or village from which we came. When the Archbishop turned to me he smiled warmly and said, "This is Elias Chacour from Gish."

"Sorry Archbishop," I spouted without thinking. "I'm not from Gish. I'm from Biram."

The room went quiet. Everyone stared at me. The Brother, the principal and the Bishop were surprised and embarrassed. *No one ever corrects an Archbishop!*

"Biram does not exist." The Archbishop snapped. This made me angry and I replied without thinking first, "But I have hope that it will exist again one day". The Archbishop held his temper with difficulty and ordered me to sit down. He quickly left the room to tour the rest of the school. Of course I suffered more days of restriction for speaking back to the Archbishop.

I thought of my mother often when studying scripture. One day when I was in Father Ghazal's class discussing how a good Christian served God, someone asked: "How could you be a good Christian if you often got angry or impatient with someone?"

Father Ghazal replied simply, "It is not enough to try to be good. You must let God occupy your body when you are challenged. It is these struggles that will tame you. When you invite God into your struggle you will be ready to do the Lord's work."

The words of my mother's prayer came back to me. She asked God to use her hands, feet and voice. I had asked God to use my hands, feet and voice too. Now Father Ghazal was saying that a servant of God is never asked to do more than that — or less.

> **You must let God occupy your Body. You must be tamed by God**

I tried to apply what I was learning about scripture to what was happening in Palestine and Israel. Was the concern in my heart for Israeli and Palestinian prompted by God? Was God calling me to not only be a priest in the Church, but also a messenger of God's love to *all* people?

I struggled with the question: "How can I deliver a message of heavenly peace to Jews and Arabs when they live daily with hate, conflict and suspicion?"

We were coming to the time when we would finish our studies at St. Joseph's and would have to decide what we would do next. Faraj and I had been friends for six years. We felt like brothers. We began to dream about our future. We would become priests and maybe serve a church together. Faraj said, "We can live simply, sharing all things in common like the early Christians. We can live peacefully among the poor. We can give our lives serving them." We talked for a long time, dreaming about the future.

The Bishop called the two of us into his office a few weeks before graduation. He told us that he had been trying to make arrangements for us to go to seminary in Jerusalem. It was with great difficulty that he told us, "You cannot go to Jerusalem. The seminary is in Jordanian territory, not Israel. The authorities will not allow you to cross the border into Jordan to go to the seminary. The Jordanians do not want 'contaminated Palestinians' from occupied territories coming to study in their sector of the city." We were stunned. What would we do now?

The Bishop was angry and was not going to let this injustice end our education. A couple of weeks later he announced, "Elias, Faraj, I have good news. I have made arrangements for you to go to seminary at Saint Sulpice in Paris."

Paris? Neither of us had been outside of Galilee except for our sheltered schooling in Haifa. What would my parents say about me going to Paris, France? I soon found out.

After graduation I went to Gish to be with my family. When I shared the news they were not sure how to respond. They were pleased one of their sons would become a priest. But, they were worried that if I went far away to Paris I might not return to my homeland. This was a very real concern because they had seen many other students go to Europe to complete their education and not return. But in the end they gave me their blessing and a week later Faraj and I boarded a ship. I left with the conviction that I would return home, regardless of the political situation, and live simply among my people.

Chapter 7

Preparing to Serve God
1958

Faraj and I arrived in Paris. The city was wonderful and much bigger and more exciting than we ever imagined. There were museums, universities, art galleries, big wonderful stores and the beautiful River Seine. We felt so privileged to be there and to study at St. Sulpice.

We had only attended a few classes when we realized we had a big problem. We only spoke a little French and could not understand what the professors were saying! We worked hard to learn the language and gradually we did.

It did not take long however before we realized that the students were uncomfortable when we talked about what was happening in our homeland. They did not want to hear about the destruction of Biram or the nearly one million Palestinians in Israel who had lost their homes and were now refugees. If we started to talk about these things they often changed the subject. Some defended the actions of the Zionists. A few even said, "There is no such thing as Palestine." Learning to relate to people with such a different viewpoint was a lesson in peacemaking. We had to remember they are children of God and we must treat them with Christ-like love.

Faraj and I talked a lot about what we hoped to do after we were ordained to be priests. We remembered that when we were in Haifa we dreamed of someday having a church together. We planned on living simply among the poor and serving them. We were going to share all things in common like the early Christians.

As the years passed and my understanding of scriptures grew, I began to wonder what was the best way to serve the church and to help my fellow Palestinians. Was it to live the quiet life Faraj and I had talked about? I began to think we should speak out and challenge people to work for reconciliation and peace.

The more we talked about it, the more I was convinced speaking out was the right way for me to serve God. Faraj decided it was not the way for him. It was an important lesson for me to learn that both Faraj and I could serve God in different ways and still both be faithful to God.

During my years at seminary I took a trip to Germany. While there I met Lony and Franz Gruber. They told me their stories about how the Jews in Germany had been persecuted and killed. I gained an appreciation for the suffering of the Jewish people at the hands of Hitler in the 1940's. Franz and Lony became close friends. As graduation drew close, I decided to make a quick trip back to Germany to see Lony and Franz and little Wolfgang, their son. I wanted to visit with them before going home to my family. When I arrived I was surprised to discover that Lony and Franz were giving me a new Volkswagen car as a going away gift! I was speechless and could not find the words to thank them. This was extraordinary generosity.

I had just learned how to drive my Volkswagen car when it was time to drive to Genoa, Italy. Then I would board a ship with my car to travel to Haifa. In July Faraj and I would meet in Nazareth for our ordination ceremony.

July came and Faraj and I found ourselves sitting together in St. Joseph's church waiting to be ordained as priests. We were both nervous. The church was full of relatives and friends. Mother and Father were seated near the front. The Brothers and students of St. Joseph's school were there. We had spent more than ten years studying in preparation for this moment. I had worked hard earning top grades and learning to speak eight languages. Our dream of becoming priests was coming true.

When the Bishop called our names, Faraj and I were presented to the congregation. As was the custom in this ceremony, the Bishop laid his hands upon us and prayed for the life of God's Spirit to fill us. Then he turned each of us to face the congregation, proclaiming, "He is worthy. He is worthy." I was filled with emotion. Would I be worthy?

Elias Chacour, the Bishop and Faraj after their ordination

After ordination I returned home to wait for the Bishop to assign me to a church. I had time to visit the upper Galilee. I had not been back to my home, Biram, since I was a boy and had a strong desire to visit. The soldiers left the village many years ago. Now no one would prohibit me from entering my true home.

I left Nazareth in the early morning in my Volkswagen. The highway wound through orchards and then started to climb over dirt and gravel roads up into the hills. I reached Biram at sun-up. I parked the car on the edge of what used to be the village square.

Then I saw a sign that said the village was a National Park and realized it had become a popular tourist site. The sign also told visitors that the inhabitants had abandoned the village of Biram! Abandoned? Not true!

It was quiet as I walked through the village except for the chirping of the birds and the crunching of the gravel under my feet. I looked at the ruined stone houses remembering the families who lived there. As I walked by the church and parish house I was overcome with sadness.

I began to remember how the village used to be. The air had been filled with talking and laughter and the scent of wood smoke from cooking. When I looked at the church and Parish House I remembered the singing and praying and the voices of the children.

> Abuna looks at the ruins of Biram and his father's orchards.

The orchard father had carefully and lovingly tended when we lived in Biram was in ruins. No one had cared for it and the grass and weeds had taken over. The trees no longer produced fruit. My special fig tree was still there. I went to it and ran my hand over the rough bark remembering all the times I climbed it and hid there.

I remembered my father's words, "The Jews and Palestinians are blood brothers and sisters. We must never forget that." The people of our village and the Jewish people from other villages traded, visited and shared a cup of coffee. They even enjoyed discussing their religious beliefs. Did not God plan that Palestinian and Jew should live together in peace in this land?

If I could restore human dignity to both Jew and Palestinian, I could work toward reconciling them. Dignity needed to be restored to both people. Justice and righteousness was what was missing. If I was going to be a true servant of God and man, I must work for justice and righteousness and be a peacemaker.

Chapter 8

Where is Ibillin?
1965

Ibillin, 2000

It was the Bishop's job to decide to which church I would be sent to be the priest. One day he called me to his office and said, "You are going to a small village of several thousand people in Galilee. The village is Ibillin." I had no idea where Ibillin was. The Bishop told me that the people there were poor and it was not an easy situation. I was to I try it for a month. He said he would give me a different assignment if it did not work out. He had notified the Responsible that I would be there by August 15.

In the hot summer heat I loaded the car and followed the map looking for the little village of Ibillin. I searched and searched among the many little villages tucked in the hills. Finally a gas station attendant gave me good directions and I found myself driving up a steep road to the village on the top of a hill.

I was eager to see the church where I would start my life's work. At last I drove into the churchyard, hot and tired from the long trip. As I stepped out of the car I heard a loud angry voice calling "Leave here! You are not wanted." I tried to tell him who I was but he would not listen and insisted I leave.

I could not believe what was happening. Certainly this could not be the Responsible — the man who cared for the grounds and building and looked after financial matters. But it was! I grabbed his hand and said, "Let's pray together." He was too surprised to speak. I did not know what would come out of my mouth, but I prayed for the church and that we could work out our differences as Christian brothers.

He took my arm and pulled me toward the church. Inside it was dark and cool. The church was uncared for. The door sagged on its hinges and benches were broken. The walls were cracked and the paint was pealing. The Responsible rambled on with accusations against the previous priest, blaming him for the condition of the church.

When he took me to the Parish House where I would live I was almost afraid to look. As I feared, it was in bad shape with two small rooms, broken furniture, and an old kerosene lamp.

Staying here was going to be a challenge. I kept telling myself, "It is only for one month." This was my assignment. This was where God had called me. I would do my best.

Ibillin was an old, old settlement. The ancestors of many of these people were active Christians as early as 325CE. Then, when Biram and many other villages were destroyed in 1951 many refugees settled in Ibillin.

I needed to find out as much as I could about the people in this small village of Christians and Muslims. I discovered that the spirit in the village was in as bad shape as the church building. The Responsible had become very powerful in the village and had even decided who should and should not come to church.

This was not right. I decided that I would stay for several months, and maybe even a year to try and bring peace to this village. I was only twenty-six years old. The Responsible had lived in the village all his life and had become very powerful. With the Responsible interfering with everything I did, how could I, a young new priest, gain the respect of the villagers? How could I bring healing to the village so that we would all respect and support one another?

I went to visit every Christian and Muslim family in the village. I wanted to know the people and for them to know me. I wanted people to know they were welcome at the church. A few of the men came to fix the broken church doors and build new benches. But most of the people were still afraid of the Responsible and would not come to church. I knew that I needed help.

I went to see an old friend in Nazareth, Mother Josephate. She was the head of a Roman Catholic community of Sisters. I asked if two of the Sisters would come and visit the women in my village once a week. She told me she had to get permission from her Superior.

When the two weeks were up I went back to Nazareth and learned the superior had refused to send the two Sisters. My disappointment turned to joy when Mother Josephate said, "He said I could not send two so I will send three."

The next Sunday I drove to Nazareth and picked up the three Sisters: Mere Macaire, Ghislaine and Nazarena. I had told the village women that the Sisters had skills in nursing and when church was over, they were welcome to bring their sick children to the Parish House. Before the day was over the three Sisters had begun to make friends with many of the village women.

Sometime later the Sisters surprised me by telling me they wanted to move to Ibillin! I was so happy. I moved out of the Parish House and gave it to the Sisters. Since I had no other place to stay, I slept in my Volkswagen car.

The Sisters and I worked hard every day visiting members of the church and other villagers, but there were still many who refused to make the effort to forgive and work for peace. I found that I was very angry with some of the people in the village. Most of all I was angry with myself because I could not do anything to change the situation.

Easter came. I had been in Ibillin for a year and a half. Even though people had anger in their hearts they would not think of missing services during the Christmas and Easter seasons. On Palm Sunday, the church was packed. It was a beautiful sunny morning. I left the doors open hoping that those who passed by might come in when they heard our singing.

When I started the service I looked out at the congregation and all I saw were angry faces. Somehow I got through the service. When it was time for the benediction. I surprised everyone. I walked to the open doors at the back of the church and shut them. From my pocket I took a thick chain, put it through the handles of the doors and fastened it with a padlock. I walked to the front of the church and said, "I love you all, but you sit here hating each other. I have done all I can to bring about reconciliation and I have failed because I am only a man. The one who can bring you together is Jesus Christ. He has the power to forgive. So now I am going to be quiet and ask Jesus to give you the power of forgiveness. We will stay here until you can and do forgive each other."

> **Those who do not love a brother or sister whom they have seen, cannot love God whom they have not seen.**
>
> 1 John 4.20

I patiently waited. The minutes passed. No one moved. Finally someone stood up. "I am sorry," he said. "I have hated my own brothers so much I wanted them to die. I have hated you. I need forgiveness."

"Of course I forgive you. Now go and make peace with your brothers," I said. He turned to his three brothers and they left their seats and rushed to him throwing their arms around him and forgiving each other. When everyone saw this, the church began to be full of noise as people asked each other for forgiveness.

For over an hour this joyful time continued with singing and people being united. I opened the doors and the celebration continued into the streets as people knocked on doors and asked to be forgiven. Ibillin was returning to life.

The Sisters and I wanted to extend this joyful spirit of forgiveness beyond our Christian community to our Muslim sisters and brothers. It began with the Sisters visiting Muslim women in their homes to get acquainted and show them that we cared for them and wanted to be their friends.

Chapter 9

Seeking Dignity and Hope
1972

The Bishop called and asked to see me. When I arrived he greeted me with a big, friendly grin. "Elias, I have great news! You have been accepted at the Hebrew University in Jerusalem to study. You will be the first Arab priest ever to attend the Hebrew University. This is a great honor. You will leave in two weeks."

I asked, "Why me? So much is happening in Ibillin and the neighboring villages!

More and more people are coming to worship on Sunday. The people are becoming reconciled in this divided land. The Sisters are starting a pre-school/kindergarten for the children. Other villages are asking if we could send Christian women to their village and start a school for their children." How could I leave? But he said, "The arrangements are made. You need to return to Ibillin and make arrangements for the church to continue its work in your absence."

When I arrived at the university I realized I was the only Arab Christian in a school of Jewish teachers and students! I wondered if I would be accepted, or again treated with suspicion and hostility because I was Palestinian. During my first semester I was amazed at how warmly I was welcomed and invited to share my viewpoints.

One of the professors, David Flusser, became a friend as well as professor to me. As we talked I realized once more that not all Jews hated Palestinians. He said to me, "God intended for the land of Israel to be a blessing for all nations — all people, not just a few." I was glad to meet someone who understood that Jews and Palestinians could get along when they begin to treat each other with dignity and respect.

Then I met my new Bishop, Bishop Joseph Raya. I learned that he had been a friend of Martin Luther King, Jr. in the 1950's when the rights of African Americans were being fought for in the United States. He prayed and marched at Martin Luther King, Jr.'s side from Birmingham to Selma to Washington D.C. He listened carefully to everything I told him about the Christians, Jews, Druze and Muslims of the Galilee and the history of Biram.

Bishop Raya became excited. "We'll stage a demonstration of our goodwill. We must rebuild the whole village of Biram," he said. Politely I explained that the government would not allow it. "They won't stop us," he said, "if we rebuild with living stones." I had thought he meant rebuilding the buildings in Biram, but he meant to rebuild the community of people of Biram. Plans were soon made to assemble fifteen hundred people for a peace gathering in Biram to show the government of Israel that Palestinians wanted only to return to their homes to live in peace.

When the day arrived we worshiped, played, ate and slept in the open for months. The news media came to report what we were doing.

Bishop Raya said to me, "We must give our Jewish brothers and sisters the chance to walk at our side. We will march to Jerusalem and show the world that we are all against violence and all we want is human dignity." Although I believed that many Jewish hearts were open to our ideas, I wondered if we would be supported in a peace march. Would those who hated Palestinians and wanted us to leave the country attack us? How much of a risk would we be taking?

On August 13, 1972, busses and cars full of people arrived on the Jaffa Road outside Jerusalem. Dozens of professors and students from the Hebrew University as well as Muslims' and Druze came to join us. Mother and father came to show me their support. Fortunately they planned to stay on the bus and pray. I was glad. I did not want them in danger if the soldiers tried to stop the march.

With a megaphone in hand I organized the marchers. As we began to walk I felt that God was with us and a calm came over me. We soon were in Jerusalem. Policemen held back thousands of spectators as we marched into the heart of the city to the Knesset. We requested a formal meeting with Prime Minister Golda Meir to discuss reconciliation between Israel and the Palestinian people.

Golda Meir said to reporters when she first came into power, "Such a thing as Palestine does not exist." We marched with the hope that she would see our numbers and be willing to talk with us. But it was not to be. We waited and waited for four days in the blistering sun of August. The doors remained closed. Bishop Raya's request to meet with Golda Meir was never granted.

As I prepared to leave, I was very discouraged that we had not been allowed to talk with Golda Meir. My spirit was lifted though when a professor stopped me and said, "Elias, are you not pleased? Look there." On the steps of the Knesset was a large group of men and women. By their dress we could tell they were Christian, Jew, Muslim and Druze. They stood with their arms around one another. "You have brought us together," the professor said. The words of the Bishop at my ordination echoed in my head. "He is worthy. He is worthy."

When I got home I was restless. I knew that something more needed to be done to restore the dignity of our people. I went to visit Bishop Raya. "How can we help our young people know they are worthwhile? They need to be productive citizens and gain self-respect. If we had good schools, that would help. But our school buildings are broken down and we have outdated books."

"Elias," said Bishop Raya, "You build the schools!" How could I do that? Was I supposed to magically produce buildings, books and teachers?

> **Elias, *you* build the schools!**

The Sisters were making an impact on the villages. In 1973 in the village of My'ilia, I was presented with an envelope full of money to make it possible for the Sisters to stay in the village and continue their work. It was wonderful that the villagers wanted to insure the education of their children by giving money, but I explained that more was needed than their money. They needed to take responsibility and get involved. I agreed to use the money to start a library with the understanding that they would build a community center where learning and fellowship would take place for the whole village. The challenge excited them and everyone began planning. Soon the idea spread to other villages. Community centers with libraries grew up in towns all around.

After some of the students I had met at the Hebrew University graduated, they told people in their hometowns about me and my attempts to help my people find hope and dignity. I began getting invitations to go to other countries and speak about my ideas about peace. I told them, "Blessed are the peacemakers…" I told them the way of peace was difficult, involving forgiveness and understanding and acceptance of your enemies. People were very interested when I talked about the schools and community centers I hoped to build throughout Galilee in an attempt to restore the dignity of my people. They gave me pledges of financial support for construction. People volunteered to come and help with the physical labor of building.

Chapter 10

Impossible Dreams?
1978

As I thought about the people of Biram and their strong desire to return to their homes, I wondered what I could do to give them hope. Even after all these years, and with the village in ruins, the families from Biram would go back and rebuild if they had the chance. I knew I could not make that happen. Then I got an idea. What if they could rebuild the church?

> This is the church as it looks today. The rest of Biram is in ruins and the people have not been able to return to live. The church may be used for weddings and funerals and families from Biram may be buried in the cemetery by the church.

I was able to get permission from the government in the fall of 1978 to restore the church. One hundred fifty young people and adults went to Biram and begin repairing and renovating the church. We were not allowed to restore any other buildings. As we worked we cheered, laughed and sang for joy. With soldiers watching us, and their guns slung over their shoulders, we built. We stood up and did something even in the face of danger. Even though we could not live in Biram, we could return here to the church to be married or to have funeral services. We would not lose touch with our land.

By this time Bishop Raya had left and I had a new Bishop. Even though I believed that building the kindergartens, community centers, and libraries were right for the church, he did not agree. He was not pleased. I found support from many friends around the world, but I was not supported by some in my own land and village. Sometimes I felt very discouraged but I knew God wanted me to remain, to follow my dreams, to continue to work for peace.

I often went from the church in Ibillin across the valley to a hill on the other side to think and pray. I was sure my Lord, my friend, my champion Jesus was with me. I sat on a rock and looked over Ibillin, the Mediterranean, Haifa and Akko. I loved the view. Most people did not come here. This hill was a garbage dump and was full of caves and wild animals. Some villagers thought that a monster lived there and called it the Monster's Mountain or the Mount of the Ogre.

One day after spending some time thinking and praying I started walking down the hill to go to my apartment on the other side of the village and realized that the church owned a piece of land on this mountain of the Ogre. I wondered if the families that owned the rest of the land would sell it to the church. I stopped and looked around me. What could I do with this land to help my people?

As I thought about this I realized that half of the residents of Ibillin were 14 years old and younger. Because there was no high school in Ibillin young people had to travel to Haifa, Akko or Nazareth to continue their education. That meant that only a few did it. Without an education they could not get good jobs. Without jobs they could not support themselves or a family. If they could get a good job they would have self-respect and dignity. The children of Ibillin needed a high school. We could build a high school on that land. That would change the name of the mountain from something negative to something positive. It would become a Mountain of Light. I decided to start talking to everyone about building a high school in Ibillin.

Although many thought my idea was a good one, they also thought it was an impossible dream. Where would the money come from?

How would we get a building permit and permission from the government? Could we purchase enough land?

I found others who wanted to build the school to include Christian, Muslim and Jewish children and teachers. But, getting a permit was a problem. Things would have been different if we had been Jewish. The government provided schools for Jewish children without question. Arabs living in Israel do not have all the same privileges as the Jews living there. Permits were almost never granted to Arabs. This is racism and oppression. It is wrong, and that is why I would not give up seeking a permit for building the school.

I tried, but I was not given a permit. My mothers' words echoed in my mind: "Always remember the children Elias. They are the most important." I decided that I would build without a permit.

Then God worked a miracle. Queen Beatrix of Holland believed that what we wanted to do was the right thing. A Christian group from Holland agreed to give us money for our project. We bought the materials and began our construction.

This caused many problems. The soldiers came many times and ordered us to stop building. They took me to court. They put our workers in jail. They threatened to destroy the building. I was taken before the judge time after time. I told the judge, "Your honor, our children's education is a serious matter, yet the authorities refuse to grant a permit to build a school. I request time to find a good lawyer. The eyes of many nations are on us. If a permit is not granted, Israel will appear in a bad light. We must not let that happen. We must build a school for our children." The judge gave us 6 months to find a lawyer. Six months! That was enough time for us to finish the school. Volunteers came from other villages and from other countries to work day and night to build the school.

The trouble was that not everyone wanted Jews and Arabs to be reconciled. There were some Jews, and some Arabs, who did not believe as I did that we should all live together in peace and share the land. They tried to stop us. Vandals came in the night and took supplies, broke windows, or turned over paint cans destroying what we had done that day. They wanted to stop us. They wanted us to be afraid.

One day as I inspected a building where there had been vandalism the night before, I grabbed the main support of a huge scaffold. As I swung myself underneath to get inside the building I heard, "Abuna! No!" Too late I realized the boys with me had seen that the support had been loosened. A large plank loaded with bricks came down on me. When I touched my throbbing head my hand came away soaked with blood. It took more than two-dozen stitches to close the gash.

There were threatening phone calls and letters. One Sunday morning there was an attempt to stab me in the back when I was leading worship. I was following the alter boys who preceded me with candles and the incense burner as I walked to the center aisle. I prayed facing the alter holding the gospel book to my forehead in reverence.

I knew something was wrong. I could hear hushed voices and the scraping of benches. I thought maybe someone was ill and was being taken out. I did not turn around because I did not want to interrupt the liturgy. I knew whatever was wrong would be taken care of by my congregation.

Later I learned that several men rushed a man out of the church because he had tried to stab me with a butcher knife.

I wanted Arab and Jew to share the land that we both loved. I challenged people to think in new ways. I did all I could to make life better for all who live in Israel and Palestine. There were Jews and Arabs who also wanted everyone to share the land. But there were Jews who believed that all of the land belonged to them and no Arabs should be in Israel. There were Arabs who were angry that they were forced off their land and into refugee camps. They believed they should be given the right to return to their homes. Others believed the Jews should leave. Violence was used by both Arabs and Jews to try to change the minds of others.

Sometimes the anger was directed at me and my building projects because they represented love for all people.

> The answer to hatred and violence is love for human beings and for life.

We did not let these incidents discourage us. We continued to build and I continued to look for ways to give our boys and girls hope.

The answer to hatred and violence is love for human beings and for life. Violence only brings more violence. So, I was determined to love those who persecuted me. I remembered that every person was born a baby in the image and likeness of God. It is only through love that the cycle of hatred and violence is broken. Love is creative, energetic, and active. Love looks for ways to restore and preserve a persons' dignity. Somehow I had to find ways to give my Palestinian brothers and sisters dignity and hope so they could have this kind of love.

On September 1, 1982 I stood on the porch of the new high school and rang a bell. With four teachers and eighty-two Muslim and Christian boys and girls from Ibillin, we began our first day at the Prophet Elias High School on the Mountain of Light.

> Today students come every day from 45 villages in a 50-mile radius to attend the high school.

We still did not have a building permit, but the judge allowed us to occupy the school without one. This meant we could not connect to water or electricity, but we decided we would manage. Then, one day in 1983 another miracle happened. The phone rang and the

man calling asked me if I still wanted a building permit. Of course I did. He told me that if I would pay him $1000 he would give me the permit. Was it a real permit I wondered? Somehow we raised the money and late in the afternoon three days later a man drove up to the school. I did not know him. He rolled down the window of his car and gave me an envelope that contained the permit. When I looked at it I knew it was authentic. I gave him the money and he drove away. I never saw him again or found out who he was.

The next dream was to build a Peace Center and place for visitors to stay when they came to help us. We were beginning to have a number of people coming to visit us from other countries. They had heard that in this troubled land, where war, persecution, occupation, and injustice dominated life, there was a special school. At this school Jews, Muslims, Christians and Druze learned to live and work together in peace.

The Peace Center and Guest House is located across the road from the high school.

We cut another level place into the side of the hill and built a Peace Center with classrooms, and a grotto for prayer on the first floor. On the top floor were bedrooms, including one for me, a kitchen and eating area.

People came from other countries to see for themselves how a Christian school in Israel with Muslim, Christian and Jewish faculty and students was possible. Many wanted to spend time with us, volunteering to do the many jobs that needed to be done to maintain our new school.

Perhaps you live in a place where it is not unusual to have a student body and faculty made up of many nationalities and religious beliefs. But in Israel such integration is not common. There are Arab Christian villages, Arab Muslim villages, Arab villages with Christians and Muslims, and there are Jewish villages. Each village has its own schools. Arabs are not allowed to live in Jewish villages and Jews do not live in Arab villages. The very large cities like Jerusalem and Haifa have Arabs and Jews living in them, but they do not mix. So, to have a private Christian school with both Arabs and Jews in the student body and on the faculty living together with respect and in peace is truly a miracle.

We soon discovered that to improve the education we were giving our children we needed to expand our buildings and programs. We needed a gymnasium and a library and more classrooms. Each time we wanted to build a building we were denied building permits but I decided to start building anyway.

Building the gymnasium was a challenge. The ground floor with several large classrooms and three-quarters of the gymnasium were finished. The workers were threatened with imprisonment. The contractor and architect were contacted personally and threatened. We had no choice but to stop.

My many attempts to obtain a permit to finish the gymnasium failed until I sought help from friends in the United States. James Baker, then Secretary of State, made it possible for me to obtain a permit from the Israeli government and we were able to finish the building.

When the high school students started to graduate they had to apply to Hebrew Universities in Israel or leave the country to study. All the universities in Israel are Jewish and only admit a small percentage of Arab students. To be admitted they must know Hebrew well enough to pass very difficult national examinations and university exams. This is one of the reasons our students are taught Arabic, Hebrew and English in elementary school. By the time they graduate from high school they are fluent in all three languages.

Our students' test scores were very high. Some were admitted to the Hebrew universities. However, those who gained admittance could not start college for two years. This is because the Jewish students have mandatory military service after high school for two years. Not everyone could afford to leave the country to study and many of those who were accepted at the Hebrew universities did not want to wait two years. Many students who left the country to study never returned. We needed these brilliant minds to stay in Israel/Palestine. Our students needed more options.

We began to dream about beginning a technical college where our students could learn skills in civil engineering, graphics, computer technology, refrigeration, and fashion design. These skills would make it possible for them to get good jobs.

The Technical College

Elementary School

We were providing such an outstanding education that people in our village wanted us to start an equally strong elementary school for their children. Although we thought this was a good idea, we did not build a building right away. We started an elementary school by using the first floor of the college building for the elementary students. The waiting list to get into the school grew quickly and we knew we had to build a building.

By the year 2004 we had built an elementary school. We started with about 560 students and had over 800 by the next year. The top floor provides guest rooms for visitors.

In 2004 we opened a small branch campus of the University of Indianapolis at Mar Elias. The students met in the college building. We hoped that someday we would have a university campus of our own.

Also in 2004 we finished a large building housing an auditorium, church, guest rooms, and meeting rooms.

The auditorium and church have become centers for the gathering of people from all over Galilee for many kinds of community events as well as campus events. This church is significant because it is the first Christian Church built in Israel in over 40 years.

The Church of the Sermon on the Mount.

The auditorium, guest rooms and meeting rooms.

At each step of the way, with each new building, we ran into opposition. There are those in the government who disagree with what we are doing. They make it difficult for us to get building permits or money to run the schools. Thankfully, there are some organizations, like Pilgrims of Ibillin in the United States, who have supported us with money and volunteers. They and many individuals have spread our story far and wide. We constantly struggle for our existence, but we will not give up! Our children deserve the best education we can give them. They deserve to live with dignity. They must learn to live in peace with their neighbors. Hopefully some of our students will help shape the future of Israel and Palestine and bring peace to this troubled land. We also hope our graduates will choose to stay in Israel/Palestine for their graduate education. By finding jobs here they can make a difference and help bring about peace.

We now have a wonderful, extraordinary campus. It is unique among schools in Israel because:

- We are a Christian school with Christians, Jews, Muslims, and Druze on the faculty, and in the student body. No person is excluded because of religion.

- Our schools are focused on teaching people to live together in peace, offering each other respect and dignity.

- We have been granted the highest academic rating of all the schools in Israel. For a private Christian institution, this is an outstanding accomplishment.

- Children and youth from 45 villages within 50 miles of Ibillin come by bus or car every day to study.

- We have developed programs and projects that bring our students together with students from Jewish schools to learn with one another.

- We offer a Regional Teacher Training Center for Arab teachers to which they can come for continuing education.

- We have developed a "gifted students' program" for the top two children from each school in the Galilee region to come for one day a week to study music, art, computers, and other enrichment programs.

- The graduates of our schools go into the world knowing what it is to live in peace with people who are different from them. They go into the world with dignity and peacemaking skills.

- In 2012 there are about 3500 students and faculty at the Mar Elias Educational Institutions.

I remember when Bishop Raya said to me, "Elias, you build the schools." It seemed impossible at the time. Our impossible dreams of building schools for our children have come true. Our God has truly blessed us. We continue to have dreams and, with the help of God and our friends around the world, they too will come true.

Chapter 11

Life at Mar Elias
2009

In the morning at 8:00am classical music is heard through loud speakers all over the campus. Making their way slowly up the hill on the narrow roads, children and youth arrive on foot, in cars, vans and buses. Their backpacks are full of books as they head for the elementary school and the high school. The campus is alive with the voices of students and teachers talking, laughing and enjoying seeing one another.

Elementary students are ready for school to start.

Every morning before the high school students go to their classes, they gather to listen for 15 minutes to one of the teachers talk to them, giving them a vision of hope.

The vision is simple: just add the letters b and r to the word *other* and you have *brother*. When we accept each other as brothers and sisters we feel whole. Christ teaches us that we are our brother's and sister's keeper.

> Every morning, students gather for 15 minutes to hear words of hope, peace and respect for one another.

During these 15 minutes we honor all the faiths present. We explain the importance of each one's special celebrations. For example: Rosh Hashanah, Yom Kippur, Sukkoth, Christmas, Easter, and Ramadan. We encourage understanding and respect of each faith.

At Mar Elias Educational Institutions our aim is to build a better future for our younger generation, whether Jew, Christian or Muslim. Our young people must understand that hatred, madness, ignorance and agony spell *destruction*. What we want is for our young people to work for *construction*. It is much harder to achieve because you need reconciliation, sacrifice, compassion, love and vision. Vision without action is a daydream. Action without vision is a nightmare. Construction is not easy, but it is the way of Christ. Jesus sacrificed himself to show us the way of love and compassion.

Does this 15 minutes make a difference in the way our students act toward one another? Does it make a difference in the way they live after they graduate? YES! We know it does. To illustrate, let me tell you some stories about our graduates.

1. One day I was on my way to court to try and get another building permit when I saw one of our graduates being led up the stairs of the courthouse by two soldiers. Worried, I called to him, "What has happened?" He answered, "It is all your fault Abuna." "My fault? Why? Tell me what is happening to you." I answered. He replied, "Every day when I was in High School, I stood with my classmates for 15 minutes each morning and listened to you and others tell us that violence just makes more violence. God does not mean for us to kill one another. I believed you. Because I am a Druze, I must go into the army. But I refuse to go to the army where I will be taught to kill. So I have been in jail for 8 months. They are taking me to see the judge to give me a chance to change my mind." I asked, "What will you do?" He replied, "8 months, plus 8 months, plus 8 months until I die. I will not bear arms to kill another human being."

2. Many of our students go into medicine. One of our Christian graduates, Michael, left Israel to go to Germany to study to be a physician specializing in cardiology. In 2005 a small Jewish girl from Nazareth needed a heart transplant. The hospital staff decided that she needed to have surgery immediately. They sent her from Israel to Germany. The physicians there are experts in that field. The surgeon was no one else but Michael.

He saved the little girl's life. He kept in touch with the parents of the little girl and they became very good friends.

3. Elias Abu Ghanima is my Godson. His father was an old friend and classmate of mine. The family has lived in Ibillin for generations. When I was the priest of the church in Ibillin little Elias would come to church early to visit with me. When he was about 13 years old I took him outside and pointed to the Mountain of the Monster and said, "Elias, you are going to graduate from the best high school in Israel over there on that mountain." I am sure he thought I was crazy. There was nothing there. He knew I did not have any money. How could this be?

During the summer before he was to enter high school he went to Haifa to take summer courses to prepare to enter a high school there. In August, when I learned what he had done, I went to Haifa. I called him out of class. I told him to get into the car and come back to Ibillin. I said to him, "You are going to attend Mar Elias High School." He did. He graduated, went to university, got his masters in English and school administration and is now the Vice Director (Vice Principal) of the high school he thought was just a crazy dream.

Vice Principal Elias Abu Ghanima.

When school starts, the students all go to their classrooms. They stay there the entire day and their teachers rotate from one room to another to teach different subjects.

There is a break for lunch, but no cafeteria. We have a couple of Kiosks on campus where the students can purchase a drink and sandwich.

Our gym provides exercise for those in the high school who have gym classes. The elementary students have an asphalt "field" on which to play.

The students do not have any elective classes in the high school or recreational after-school activities. It is not that we don't want to offer them, but that we don't have money to provide them. Students go home after school and do their homework and help their parents.

Our students take their education so seriously that all of our students who start high school graduate. Our graduates have to take national exams to be eligible to apply for university. The graduates of Mar Elias High School consistently have some of the highest scores of any school in Israel. Four times we have had students achieve perfect scores.

In 2006 we were reminded of the academic achievements of our high school graduates. There is a university in Haifa, The Technion, that is very prestigious and highly rated in Israel. We received a letter from them asking us to submit the names of several students we would like to recommend to attend this university. We submitted the names of eight brilliant students. Several thousand students from all the schools in Israel applied. If admitted the students would receive full scholarships. Our eight students went to take the very difficult entrance exams. Five of our students were accepted. Can you imagine how proud we were that out of the 25 students in all of Israel that were accepted, five of them were from Mar Elias?

These stories are proof for me that all the studying, the struggles with authorities for permits, all the other difficult times I went through were worth it. Change does not come quickly, but it can come. My dreams became a reality and yours can too.

Chapter 12

Hope for the Future

Well my friends, that is my story. Did I know when I was seven years old, climbing my favorite fig tree, or playing with my friends, or sitting on my mother's lap listening to stories from the Bible that I would grow up to be a peacemaker? No, I did not.

Do you know right now what you will do with the rest of your life? It is never too late to start making decisions that will lead you to live a life that serves your God. As you can see from my story, it is not always easy to live the life of a peacemaker. But I pray that you will try. You can begin being a peacemaker right now.

When I started my story I said that I was an Arab Palestinian Christian and an Israeli Citizen. Now that you have read my story, I hope you understand each part of my identity.

Arab — My native language is Arabic.
Palestinian — I was born in Palestine.
Christian — My family has been Christian since the time of the first Christians.
Israeli Citizen — I live in Ibillin, which is located in the State of Israel, so I am a citizen of Israel and carry an Israeli passport.

How would you describe your identity? However you describe it, I hope you are proud of who you are and that you will follow in the footsteps of Jesus. If you do, you can make life better for those around you and be a peacemaker.

I travel to many places around the world to tell the story of the Palestinian people and what has happened to them, and the struggle of the Israelis to establish a homeland. Often people get upset because the conflict between the Palestinians and the Israeli government has been going on for so many years. Sometimes the situation seems hopeless.

Often people ask me, "Where is the hope Abuna?" I tell them that the hope for the future is in each one of them, and especially in the children. ***I tell you, my hope is in YOU.*** Let God use your hands and your tongue to work for justice and peace in your family, school, church, and community.

Are there times when you find yourself being treated unfairly or need courage to stand up for what is right? I have felt this way many times. During these times I remember some of my favorite Bible passages and the teachings of Jesus. I share them here hoping you will remember them and they will give you the strength to be a peacemaker.

> ### *The Beatitudes:*
> The beatitudes have become one of my favorite passages of scripture. This passage guides me in everything I do. When I understand Jesus' words in his native Aramaic language, I translate like this:
>
> "Get up, go ahead, do something, move, you who are hungry and thirsty for justice, for you shall be satisfied."
>
> "Get up, go ahead, do something, move, you peacemakers, for you shall be called children of God."
>
> The beatitudes are a command to get busy and work for justice.
>
> I shared what I had learned in my language studies about the translation of the Beatitudes with my friend, The Rev. Dr. Donald Griggs. He wrote the following. I believe his words reflect my thinking and the original meaning of the Beatitudes accurately.

God calls you to get up and move, you who are poor in spirit, for yours is the kingdom of heaven.

Straighten up, you people who grieve, for you will be comforted.

Lift your head, you people whose hearts are humble, for you will inherit the earth.

Set yourself in a new direction, you who hunger and thirst for righteousness, for you will be filled.

When you do acts of mercy, you will receive mercy.

When you act as persons whose hearts are pure, you shall see God. Commit yourself to be a peacemaker, not a peace contemplator, and then you will be called children of God.

Do the right thing and then the kingdom of heaven will be yours. You are to act with courage and integrity in response to those who insult you, mistreat you, and tell evil lies about you because of your faith in Jesus Christ.

Born Babies:
People are not born Christian, Jew, Muslim, American, German, Mexican, or a police or military person. Everyone is just born a baby in the image and likeness of God. When we meet someone who is hostile towards us we must remember that we are facing a father, son, daughter, wife, mother, sister or brother who is a human being just as we are. Treating people with respect, dignity and love helps to give them a chance to put their hostility to the side and show respect for others.

Violence and War:
War only creates more widows and orphans. Violence escalates violence.

God does not kill. Whenever there is killing or oppression it is we who do it. God is the one persecuted and is the victim of our bad deeds. God gives life. God forgives and goes beyond justice to compassionate love.

The Jews:
I do not hate the Jewish people. Hatred is corruption. I will always protest every evil act against me or my people, regardless of who does it. But I will never protest with violence. I will not return hatred because it will only increase hatred.

If you support the Palestinian cause, that is wonderful. But if that means you hate the Jews, we do not want your support. We do not need that kind of friendship. Reach out to the Jews in your community and get to know them. They need your friendship as much as we do. They are suffering too. Work toward reconciliation and justice for all and you will be working for peace.

Respecting human rights and protecting human life should arise out of one's love for human beings and for life.

Peace:
We do not need peace *contemplators*. Contemplators sit and think, but don't do anything.

We need peace*makers*. Peacemakers get busy and do something.

Tolerance and Acceptance:
I do not "tolerate" anyone. To tolerate is to put up with something or someone you don't agree with until what bothers you changes or goes away. You endure and resist the action of someone else. When you tolerate someone you are not fully accepting him or her. But, when you accept someone you are not looking for him or her to change. You accept all that a person is with

all their shortcomings and faults as well as their gifts and talents. You see them as children of God.

Think about how you make decisions. Take advantage of all the wonderful opportunities you have for learning. Think about how you treat other people. Remember that every person you meet was born a baby in the image and likeness of God. They may not treat you as a child of God, but that does not excuse you from treating them as God's creation. Jesus told us to love one another as we love ourselves.

God has led me since I was a little boy in a small, poor Christian Arab village to believe deeply in my companion, Jesus the Christ. Jesus' teachings have led me to care deeply for all of God's creation. That caring has resulted in working hard to bring justice, peace, dignity and hope to all the people living in Israel and the Palestinian territories.

You may feel powerless to bring change to your part of the world, but you are not. Start with the people who are around you. Dream. Then work to make your dreams come true.

A Note to Parents and Teachers

This book was written in response to requests from parents for a book about Abuna that they could read and discuss with their children. At the same time we were receiving these requests, churches connected to Pilgrims of Ibillin were asking for a resource they could use in their Vacation Church School or during Church School to tell Father Chacour's story and teach about peacemaking.

Consequently, the book you hold in your hands is not a novel, but is a teaching tool intended for adults and children/youth to read the stories together, discuss them, pray together, and discover how they can become more effective peacemakers in their world.

The questions that are provided for each chapter will help start the discussions.

The section: *Words and Facts* should be referred to frequently to define words used in the text and to develop a better understanding of the situation in Israel/Palestine.

It is our hope that a dialogue between adults and children/youth will inspire both to discover ways they can become peacemakers and make a difference in our world as they follow our Lord, Jesus the Christ.

Questions To Think About and Discuss

Chapter 1
- Elias described his town of Biram with fruit trees, a village square, his church and the homes of many relatives. How would you describe where you live? What does your town / city look like?
- Who lives in your home? Where do your relatives live?
- Elias was happy and at peace in his village. What makes you feel happy and at peace?
- What are some things you can do to be helpful to other members of your family and make your home a more comfortable, happy place to live?

Chapter 2
- The Chacour family roasted a lamb for special celebrations. What are the special foods your family prepares for celebrations?
- Elias and his brothers and sister were excited to sleep on the roof of the house. Have you ever slept outside under the stars? If so, what do you remember that made it special?
- The news about Hitler killing the Jews was terrible. Has there been a time when your family learned very bad news? What did you do?
- Why do you think Rudah was scolded for bringing a gun into the house?
- What causes you to become angry? What causes you to become afraid?
- Elias's father told his children, "We do not use violence EVER even if someone hurts us." Do you agree with this? Why? Why not?

Chapter 3
- Strangers came to Biram and used their power to make the people leave their homes. If you were forced from your home, where do you think your family would go?

Blessed are the Peacemakers

- There are many places in the world that have been, or are now being invaded by soldiers from another country. What wars are going on right now? What is happening to the people who have been attacked?
- People around the world work to help those who are suffering because of war or natural disaster. What are some things people in your community are doing to help people who are suffering? How can you become involved?
- People are challenged to find ways to be peacemakers when there is injustice. As a Christian, what are some things you and other Christians in your community can do when you see injustice happening?

Chapter 4

- Are there refugees or homeless people in your community? Who are they? What are some ways you and your family can be of help to these people?
- Elias says that the prayers he prayed telling God to use his hands, feet and tongue, were the most important prayers of his life, and the first small step on the journey toward becoming a peacemaker. Why do you think those prayers were so important?
- What do you think it means to let God use your hands, feet, and tongue?
- Elias and his family pray often. How would you explain to someone else what is prayer?
- When do you pray? Do you pray:
    To give thanks?
    To ask for forgiveness?
    When you are sad?
    When you want something to happen?
    To praise God?
  Add other situations that cause you to pray.

Chapter 5

- Why do you think Elias' parents sent him to an orphanage for an education when that would mean sending him away from the family for many years?

- Father told Elias that to be a true man of God he would have to learn how to reconcile enemies and turn hatred into peace. What do you think he meant by that?
- If you were Elias, and learned that soldiers had destroyed not only your home but also the whole village, how do you think you would feel and respond?
- Elias felt more anger than he had ever experienced when he learned what the soldiers did to Biram. When are some times you have been very angry? How did you express your anger? What are some ways you can use your anger in a non-violent way to bring about peace?

Chapter 6
- Faraj offered friendship to Elias. What did Faraj do to become friends with Elias? How do you become a close friend to someone?
- When are some times you feel close to God? Describe how you feel when you are aware of the presence of God.
- How do you think people who live with hate and conflict can learn to live in peace?
- Elias and Faraj experienced rejection and obstacles to their future because they were Palestinians. Are there people in your school or community who experience injustice because of their race, religion, or place in society? If so, what are some things you can do to show them your friendship?

Chapter 7
- Elias and Faraj discovered they could both serve God, but in different ways. How did Faraj want to serve God? How did Elias want to serve God? What was the difference?
- How do people you know serve God?
- In what ways do you serve God?
- People must experience justice and righteousness to get along together. What do the words "Justice" and "Righteousness" mean?
- Elias decided that to be a man of God he must be a peacemaker. Is serving God the same thing as being a peacemaker? If so, how? If not, why?

Chapter 8
- Abuna Elias Chacour talks about the conflicts and hatred in the village. Where do you see conflicts happening? What are some of the causes of the conflicts?
- What are some ways you can work to help resolve conflicts and bring about peace?
- Are there conflicts in your family? What are some things you can do to resolve the conflicts?
- Is there someone you don't like because they have different ideas than you do? What are some things you can do to change how you feel about that person and how you treat him or her?
- When the people let Jesus into their hearts they were able to forgive each other. Think about what it means to forgive someone. How can you let Jesus into your heart to help you forgive someone who has hurt you?

Chapter 9
- Elias went to the Hebrew University wondering if he would be accepted. Are there places where you are afraid you will not be accepted? If so, what can you do to change the situation?
- What are some reasons Bishop Raya's idea for a march might be dangerous?
- Why do you think people took the risk to join him?
- In what ways do you think participating in the march and helping to build schools, libraries and community centers gave people hope and dignity?
- Bishop Raya and Elias both talk about "living stones." What do you think they mean by "living stones"?
- Make a list of some ways you and your friends can work to change laws and rules so the rights of all people are respected.
- When Bishop Raya told Elias to build the schools, it seemed like an impossible task. Have you ever been asked to do something that you thought you could not do but discovered you could?

Chapter 10
- Abuna Elias Chacour has worked to bring hope and dignity to the lives of the Palestinian people and reconciliation and understanding between Arab and Jew. Many in the government of Israel, and some Arabs oppose him. What do you think are

some reasons why he has had the courage to do what he thought was right?
- What are some dreams you have for your future? What steps do you need to take to make your dreams come true?
- What are some things you are going to do to become a peacemaker?

Chapter 11
- Abuna tells us some stories about the graduates of the high school. Choose a story. What do you think the story is telling you about living as a peacemaker? How do you think the education at the Mar Elias schools influenced the person in your story?
- What do you think Abuna means by the statement:

    "Hatred, madness, ignorance and agony spell *destruction. Construction* is much harder to achieve because you need reconciliation, sacrifice, compassion, love and vision."

    Why do you think he says that construction is harder to achieve than destruction?
- There are many people in this book who are peacemakers besides Abuna Chacour. Make a list of the ones you remember. Think about why you chose them. In what ways do you want to be like them?

Chapter 12
- How would you describe your identity?
- Abuna shares some Bible passages and teachings of Jesus that are guidelines for the way he makes decisions and lives his life. Look at these passages and teachings and choose one that you like. What do you like most about it?
- How do you think these thoughts or guidelines can help you be a peacemaker?
- Which of these thoughts or guidelines do you think would be the hardest to follow? Why?
- Which one of these guidelines do you want to remember and live by?
- When you think about the way you treat others, is there something you need to change in order to be more like a peacemaker?

WORDS and FACTS

Abuna
Abuna is the Arabic word for "Father." Father Elias Chacour is often addressed as Abuna Chacour, or sometimes just, Abuna.

Arab
Arab people originally came from countries in the Middle East. Today they live in the Middle East and in many other countries. The native language of the Arab people is Arabic. Arabs born in other countries than the Middle East may or may not speak Arabic. Some of the Arab countries in the Middle East are: Iraq, Saudi Arabia, Egypt, Syria, Sudan, Jordan, Lebanon, Palestine, Morocco, Algeria and Tunisia.

Arab Christians
Some Arabs are Christians. Arab Christians live all over the world including the State of Israel and the Palestinian Occupied Territories. Arab Christians from Palestine trace their heritage back to the time of Jesus.

Archbishop
An Archbishop has authority over the bishops, priests and churches in a geographical area. In 2006, Elias Chacour was appointed the Archbishop of the Melkite Catholic Church of the Galilee. This is the largest Christian community in the Holy Land.

Archbishop Elias Chacour

Biram
Biram is a small Palestinian village in the region of Galilee just south of the Lebanon border. Biram is the village in which Father Chacour and his family lived until the villagers were forced out of the village in 1948. Jewish Zionist soldiers destroyed Biram in 1951.

Bishop
A Bishop has the authority to oversee the priests of churches in a geographical area called a diocese.

Brother
There are three ways the word "Brother" is used in the story. 1) Male family members. 2) Jews, Christians and Muslims are "brothers" (and "sisters") because they claim Abraham as their ancestral father. 3) Men belonging to a religious order at the seminary Elias attended were called "Brothers."

Christian
Christians are those people who believe that Jesus is the Son of God who was crucified and has risen from the dead. Jesus' life and teachings are the standards by which Christians live in relationship to others and God.

Druze
Druze is a religion that has its roots in Islam. Druze are secretive about their beliefs so we don't know a lot about them. In Israel, the Druze are required to serve in the military because Druze swear allegiance to the government of the country in which they live.

Galilee
The region in the north of Israel between the Sea of Galilee and the Mediterranean Sea, north to the border of Lebanon and south to Mount Carmel. Jesus lived in Nazareth as a child in the Galilee region and traveled in this area teaching, preaching and healing the people.

Grotto

A grotto is a cave in the side of a hill. The mountain on which the schools have been built had many caves. When the Guesthouse was built, access to a grotto was made possible. The grotto was made into a place of worship with candles and other religious items. A bench was carved out of the wall on which to sit.

Worshipping in the Grotto in the Guest House.

Heritage

The heritage of an individual is the history, traditions, possessions, property, morals, values and customs passed on from one generation to another. Families have a heritage and nations have a heritage.

Ibillin

Ibillin is a small Arab village of Christians and Muslims in the Galilee region of Israel. This is the village where Father Elias Chacour became priest of the St. George Melkite Catholic Church in 1965.

Ibillin, 2005

Since then, Father Chacour has established schools in Ibillin to which Christians, Muslims, Jews and Druze children come from 45 towns and villages around Ibillin.

Islam

The prophet Mohamed founded the religion of Islam. The people who follow this religion are called Muslims. Many of them live in the

State of Israel and the Palestinian Occupied Territories. Muslims also live in many other countries.

Israel
Israel was the name God gave to Jacob (Genesis 35.10). The descendants of Jacob were called Israelites. In 1948 the United Nations divided Palestine to create a homeland for the Jews. Some of the land was established as the State of Israel and some became Palestinian Territories. The boundaries within this "Holy Land" and the governments that have ruled them have changed many times throughout Biblical and modern history.

Israeli
An Israeli is a citizen of the State of Israel. An Israeli citizen may be Jewish, Christian, Muslim or Druze. Father Chacour is an Arab Israeli citizen who is also a Palestinian by heritage.

Israeli Defense Force
The Israeli army.

Judaism
The religion of Judaism dates back to the time of Abraham. Jesus and his followers were Jews. For many years Jews have lived all over the world without a country to call their own. In 1948 the United Nations established the State of Israel in Palestine for the Jews to have a homeland.

Kindergarten
At Mar Elias Educational Institutions children enter Kindergarten at age three and graduate to first grade in the Elementary school when they are six.

Knesset
The name given to the body of people ruling the government of Israel.

Languages
Three languages are common in Israel and Palestine:
- *Hebrew* (spoken by the Jews),
- *Arabic* (spoken by the Arabs) and
- *English* (a universal language).

At Mar Elias Educational Institutions all three languages are taught beginning in elementary school. By the time they are in high school they know all three languages.

They learn all three languages because: (1) Father Chacour wants all his students to be able to communicate with all their neighbors. (2) Students graduating from High School must take national exams to qualify for University studies. The exams are given in Hebrew because the schools are located in the Jewish State of Israel and instruction in the Universities is given in Hebrew.

Mar Elias Educational Institutions
This is the name given to the group of schools Father Chacour founded. "Mar" is an Arabic word for "Prophet" and "Elias" is Arabic for "Elijah". Mar Elias means Prophet Elijah. The schools are named after the prophet Elijah who served God in the same region where Ibillin is located.

Maronite Catholic Church
The church is named for its founder, St. Maron. It is known for actively working for human rights, the development of democratic institutions, the promotion of women's status in society and reconciliation of the Lebanese people. There are Maronites in many countries. They have a strong loyalty to Lebanon.

Melkite Catholic Christians

The name Melkite comes from the Arabic word meaning "king." In the early days of the Christian Church there was a disagreement between the King of Byzantium and the Pope about who was Jesus.

St. George Melkite Catholic Church in Ibillin

Some people thought the King of Byzantium had the right interpretation. Some thought the Pope did. Those who believed the same as the King were called Melkites (Kings men).

The Pope in Rome governs the Roman Catholic Church. The Synod and the Patriarch govern the Melkite Catholic Church. Father Elias Chacour is a priest in the Melkite Catholic Church.

Muslim – See *Islam*

Orphan – Orphanage

An orphan is someone whose mother and father are not living, or whose parents cannot care for their children. An orphanage is a place where many orphans live and are cared for until someone wants to adopt a child. The orphanage where Elias went to receive his education did not offer children for adoption. The children stayed until they were 15 years old. Elias Chacour was not an orphan, but the Bishop let him live in the orphanage so that he could receive an education.

Occupied

The word "occupied", when referring to The Palestinian Territories, describes the activity of the Israeli Defense Force and

Israeli government of using force to control the land and government of the Palestinian people. One way this is being done is by building a giant wall between Israel and Palestine and around Palestinian cities (such as Bethlehem) and establishing checkpoints through which everyone must pass. The ability to pass through is at the discretion of Israeli soldiers. The Israeli government is building the wall to protect themselves from attacks by the Palestinians.

Palestinian Territories
In 1948 the United Nations decided to partition Palestine into two states — a Palestinian state for the Palestinians and a Jewish state for the Jews. There has been a lot of controversy about where the boundaries should be. The Wall being built by Israel is not being built on the boundaries designated by the United Nations. The wall is often built on Palestinian land isolating villages and cities and between homes and orchards or businesses.

Palestinians
Palestinians are all the Arab people who have lived in the land that is now Israel and the Palestinian Occupied Territories for generations dating back hundreds of years before Christ. Palestinians living in the State of Israel are Israeli citizens, but are often governed by different laws and have fewer opportunities than Jewish people who live in Israel. Those who live in the Palestinian Occupied Territories live with Israeli laws that are enforced by Israeli soldiers who occupy the territory.

Parish House
A building owned by the church and used as a residence for the Priest and/or a school for the children. In Biram the Parish House was where Elias and the other children went to school. In Ibillin the Parish House was where the Priest lived. Later, Abuna turned the house over to the Sisters to live in. When the Sisters started the pre-school/kindergarten they used the Parish House.

Persecuted
To persecute someone is to make him or her suffer because of religious beliefs, race, or political convictions.

Pilgrims of Ibillin
Pilgrims of Ibillin is an organization located in the United States and dedicated to the support of Christian mission projects in Israel. They work primarily to raise money to support the Mar Elias Educational Institutions and other organizations with similar goals in Israel and Palestine. They are committed to working for peace and justice for all people.

Refugee
People become refugees when their homes have been destroyed or taken from them by force. In this story the refugees fled from danger, sometimes traveling to another country to escape being killed or persecuted. These people were forced out of their homes so quickly they took only those things they could carry with them. Members of the Chacour family are refugees because even today they are not allowed to live in their hometown of Biram. Some people become refugees because their homes were destroyed by natural disasters such as floods, earthquakes or fire.

Religions
The primary religions found in Israel and the Palestinian Territories are Jewish, Muslim, Christian and Druze.

Settlements
Settlements are new communities, built for Jews in the Palestinian Occupied Territories by the state of Israel on land owned by Palestinians. The settlements provide modern and beautiful homes, parks and recreation. Fences and guards protect the settlements.

Beautiful Jewish settlements (cities) sit high on the hills.

Special highways are built connecting the settlements and the State of Israel. Arabs are not allowed to use them.

Shalom and Salam These words mean "peace" in Hebrew (Shalom) and Arabic (Salam). They appear on a retaining wall at Mar Elias educational Institutions reminding the students to live together in peace.

Sister
The word "Sister" is used three ways, 1) a relative. 2) A women who belongs to a religious order. 3) When referring to Arab Christians, Muslims and Jews being "brothers and sisters" because they all claim Abraham as their ancestral father.

Zionist A group of Jewish people, some of whom are dedicated to establishing an all-Jewish nation. It was Zionist soldiers who destroyed Biram and 450 other Palestinian villages between 1948 and 1951. Homes continue to be destroyed today. Not all Jewish people are Zionists.

Archbishop Elias Chacour — Awards and Accomplishments

In addition to the accomplishments you have read about in the story, Father Chacour has done much to fulfill the statement at his ordination, "He is Worthy. He is Worthy."

He has been the founder of, or assisted in the founding of the following:
- The first Arab Students' Hostel in Jerusalem.
- Mariam Bawardi Youth and Adult Center in Ibillin
- Mariam Bawardi Kindergarten
- Community and youth Center in Maylia
- Saint John Chrysostomus Secondary School and Youth Center in Gish
- Saint Joseph Community Center and Youth Center in Tarshiha
- Boy Scouts Center in Shefa'amr
- Community Center in Fassuta
- Community Center in Isifya
- Eight public libraries
- A summer camp for children that grew from 1129 to more than 5000 young people of different religions and denominations from thirty different villages in the Galilee region.
- School of Arts and Technology for gifted children.
- Mar Elias Teachers' Regional Resource Center for continuing education of Arab teachers in the Galilee.

Father Chacour has also received many awards including:
- World Methodist Peace Award — 1994
- Chevalier de la Legion d'Honneur by the President of France — 1999
- Marcel Rudloff Peace and Tolerance Award at Strasbourg — 2000

- Niwano Peace Award, Tokyo-Japan — 2001
- Man of the Year in Israel — 2001
- International First Freedom Award from the Council for America's First Freedom, Richmond Virginia — 2005

In addition he has been nominated for the Nobel Peace Prize three times — 1984, 1989 and 1994

Since his ordination in 1965:
- He has earned degrees from the Hebrew University (where he was the first Arab student to study the Bible and the Talmud) and the University of Geneva.
- He has been awarded honorary degrees from St. Michael's College in Winooski, Vermont, Texas Wesleyan University at Fort Worth, Duke University at Durham, North Carolina, Indianapolis University and Emory University, Atlanta, and Ecumenical Theological Seminary, Detroit, Michigan.
- In February of 2006, he accepted the appointment by the Melkite Catholic Church to the position of Archbishop of Haifa, Akko, Nazareth and all Galilee. He is the first native-born Palestinian in two hundred years to hold this position and the first Israeli citizen ever to hold this position.

Archbishop Elias Chacour

Pilgrims of Ibillin
www.pilgrimsofibillin.org

Pilgrims of Ibillin Mission Statement

Pilgrims of Ibillin is dedicated to the support of Christian communities in Israel and their efforts to promote peaceful coexistence with Jews and Muslims. We work primarily in partnership with Mar Elias Educational Institutions, founded by Father Elias Chacour, in the village of Ibillin, in the Galilee region. Our support is through financial contributions, sponsorship of pilgrimages, and interpretation of the vision of MEEI. We seek to foster greater understanding of issues related to Christians, Muslims, and Jews in the Holy Land.

The Pilgrims of Ibillin:
- Establishes local chapters in various places in the United States.
- Conducts fund raising events.
- Provides resources: brochures, books, a video and DVD
- Interprets the mission of MEEI and Pilgrims of Ibillin when and where invited.
- Produces and distributes a newsletter three times a year.
- Maintains a web site at www.pilgrimsofibillin.com
- Sponsors visits of representatives of MEEI to the United States

You Can Help by:
- Becoming informed by reading books by Father Chacour, and other current publications.
- Adding your name to the mailing list to receive the newsletter from Pilgrims of Ibillin.
- Working with five or more persons in your church or community to form a local chapter of Pilgrims of Ibillin. Contact the Executive Director for more information.

- Sharing information and resources about the Mar Elias Educational institutions in Ibillin and about issues related to the conflicts in Palestine and Israel.
- Checking out our website at www.pilgrimsofibillin.org
- Making a contribution to Pilgrims of Ibillin to support the work of Father Chacour and his colleagues at the Mar Elias Schools.
- Having a fund raising event at your church.

Resources available from Pilgrims of Ibillin:

Books: *Blood Brothers*, Elias Chacour with David Hazard,
We Belong to the Land, Elias Chacour with Mary E. Jensen,
Blessed Are The Peacemakers, Archbishop Elias Chacour and Patricia R Griggs

DVD's: *A Man of Galilee.* 23 minutes. Learn about the life of Father Chacour, the development of the school and the impact of the political situation in Israel.
Building Peace on Desktops. 12 minutes. Students, faculty and Archbishop Chacour speak about the teachings of hope, love, peace and respect for one another that is taught at MEEI.

Pilgrims Post: A newsletter from Pilgrims of Ibillin is available via hard copy or e-mail.

To request resources, to be added to the mailing list, or to make contributions to Pilgrims of Ibillin, please go to www.pilgrimsofibillin.org.

Pilgrims of Ibillin is a 501(c)(3) not for profit corporation. Contributions are acknowledged and are tax deductible.